# Leveraging New Paradigms for Enhanced Mobile Network Security

## Sanobar

# CONTENTS

# Chapter 1

# INTRODUCTION

Mobile access to the Internet is becoming a fundamental need in modern life; mobile devices have outnumbered human population for the last few years [1–3]. Mobile Network Operators (MNOs) have been challenged to keep up with the rate of growth of mobile traffic, while still attempting to remain profitable. The end users' constant expectation for lower data costs, while still expecting improvements in data transfer rates as well as Quality of Service (QoS), has led to the need to lower the cost per bit for the users. In order to achieve this MNOs are now making use of new paradigms in order get higher levels of throughput from their networks, which has led to the Mobile Network (MN) being a more enticing target for malicious actors. The inclusion of the new paradigms also brings the opportunity to leverage off their functionalities to improve the overall security of the MN. These paradigms allow for attacks against the MN to be mitigated in a proactive and automated way.

Creating secure mobile networks has been a goal since its inception and security concerns have significantly influenced its design. Focus has been on ensuring that the mobile network is protected from threats by malicious end users or attackers. Threats to the mobile network can be classified into the following categories [4]:

1. Rendering a system unreliable or unusable.

2. Performing unauthorised manipulation of information.

3. Obtaining unauthorised access to information

4. Theft of service.

5. Losing control of the network or node within the network

Current mobile networks are comprised of a Radio Access Network (RAN) and a Core Network (CN). End users access the mobile network via the RAN. The CN is then responsible for processing and administrating over the user's service (e.g. ensuring QoS and monitoring network usage for accounting purposes) as well as connecting to backhaul networks such as the Internet. The CN is also referred to as the Evolved Packet Core (EPC) and these terms will be used interchangeably. The EPC is the CN of the fourth generation of mobile networks (4G).

Research focus has been on preventing an attacker from gaining access to the EPC by defending the perimeter nodes, essentially trusting all internal entities within the EPC. This trusting network is shown in Figure 1.1 where all entities can communicate with one another. The "perimeter only" approach and trust level has been demonstrated not to be effective for a variety of reasons [5]. Methods/vulnerabilities still exist that could allow the attacker to find themselves with administrative level access to a node in the EPC. Examples of such methods can be found in List 1.1

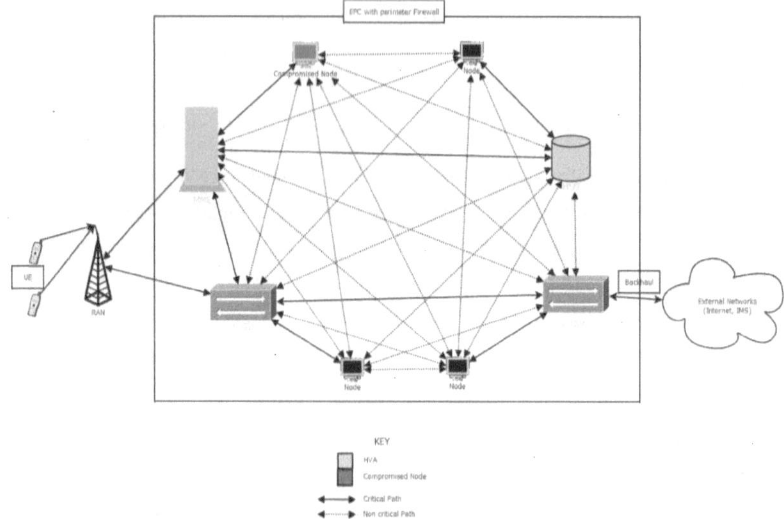



Figure 1.1: Illustration of EPC configuration differentiating between critical and non critical paths

List 1.1: Examples of Network Vulnerabilities

- Social engineering techniques to obtain an MNO employee's credentials (i.e. phishing).

- Configuration error on a node or the services running on a node, leading to the ability for Remote Code Execution (RCE).

- Malware being loaded onto the node via a patch or update of a compromised third party application via a supply chain attack [6, 7].

- Insecure code being deployed onto a node.

- Attacks using vulnerabilities and exploits not predicted by the creators of the security procedures.

Attackers are considered to be any actor that is targeting the EPC with malicious intent. Attackers can range from individual actors all the way up to a nation state organisation that specializes in Advanced Persistent Threats (APT) against information systems such as a MN. This research covers attackers that are considered to be any actor that is able to exploit vulnerabilities in computer systems to take control of an entity in the EPC. The attackers aim to garner more control or information from the EPC by laterally moving to other nodes within the network.

If an attacker were to gain access to a node in the EPC, all perimeter protection mechanisms, such as firewalls, would not be effective at warning the MNO that an attacker has successfully infiltrated their EPC. Once an attacker has established a base inside the network, the next step would be for the attacker to perform reconnaissance on the network to locate High Value Assets (HVA) or other vulnerable nodes in the network [8]. An example of such attack on an HVA presented in this research is for an attacker to target the Home Subscriber Server (HSS) which is the main database of the EPC in order to exfiltrate all the information that it contains. Other HVAs in the EPC contain all users data or could be used to perform a Man In The Middle (MITM) attack on all traffic through the mobile network. It is evident that the current EPC design requires security systems put in place that can protect it from attacks originating from other nodes within the EPC.

Figure 1.1 illustrates the network pathways that are open within the mobile EPC for an attacker to use in order to laterally move throughout the network. The large amount of non critical network paths between nodes within the EPC only gets exponentially larger as more nodes are added to the EPC. Non critical network paths are paths between nodes that never need to communicate with one another. In a typically functioning CN, non critical paths should never get used. The attacker on a compromised node within the EPC would be able to make use of any of the paths to get access to another entity within the network thereby ensuring that their attack can be persistent as the attacker has many points of control. These paths would

4

be considered open as each of the nodes in the EPC are connected to the same Local Area Network (LAN) segment, which is required for the critical paths to be available.

Figure 1.1 also shows the compromised node as an administrative node on the EPC, these nodes are included in the EPC in order for MNO technical staff to gain access to the EPC so that they can perform administrative tasks or reconfigure the EPC. The admin nodes (also known as jump boxes) are the nodes most likely to get compromised because they experience the most human interaction which can lead to human error and the possible introduction of vulnerabilities [9, 10]. These nodes would also be the entry point for attackers that have been successful in phishing for credentials.

Data flows between network entities make use of the network paths between the entities and are the flows that are referred to throughout this work. Any communication between network entities requires a flow of data between the two network entities along a network path. For the rest of this research, a malicious flow can be defined as any flow that make use of a non critical path because these paths would never get utilised during normal operations of the EPC, therefore data traversing these non critical paths must be seen as suspicious.

Network Intrusion Detection Systems (NIDS) such as Snort [11] and Surricata [12] have been designed to detect suspicious reconnaissance behaviours such as network mapping to gain information on the IP addresses and configuration of nodes in the network. Current IDS lack the ability to distinguish between flows that make use of critical or non critical paths within a network. So if an attacker already knows the IP address of an HVA, current IDS systems would not get triggered by what would seem to be a legitimate lateral movement from a compromised node to an HVA. This is due to the fact that if two nodes exist in the same LAN segment with open ports, then the nodes would be able to communicate with one another. Figure 1.2 illustrates a compromised node on the network attempting to access the HSS on

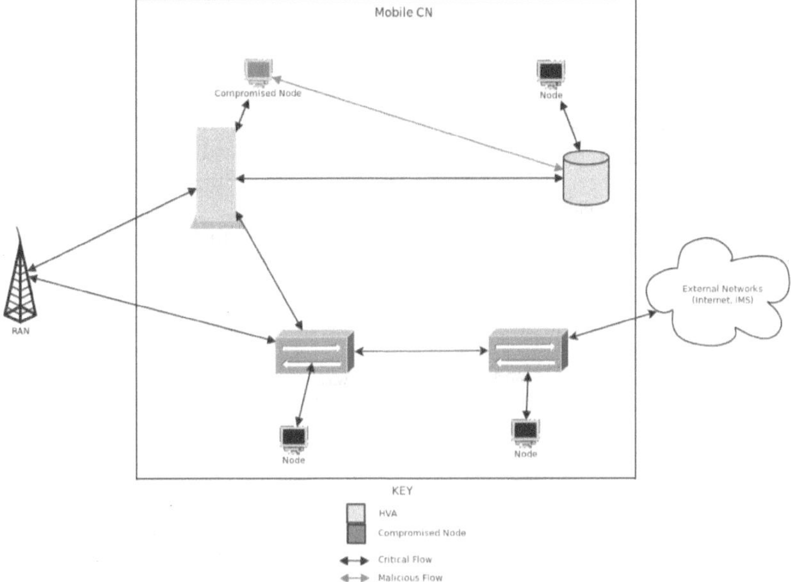

Figure 1.2: Attacker successfully achieving a malicious flow to an HVA of the mobile core network

the EPC. This network path (red path) allows for a flow that is not critical to the functionality of the network so this flow should be seen as suspicious/-malicious.

The ability to distinguish between critical and non-critical paths requires a network wide, high level of abstraction and management in order to strictly define which flows are critical to the functionality of the EPC. Software Defined Networking (SDN) has been proposed to provide a high level abstraction, view and control over networks. In a network that makes use of the SDN paradigm, a logically centralized controller would be able to distinguish between malicious and critical flows within the EPC.

SDN requires the switches that connect the EPC elements together to be enabled with a specific protocol that allows communications between the switches and a central controller, such as OpenFlow [13]. With SDN implemented in a network, the switches become simpler devices that only forward traffic based on a flow table that gets populated by the logically centralised controller [14]. When a new flow is requested of a switch that is not already in the switch's flow table, the switch then reaches out to the controller, via the OpenFlow protocol, with the request of how to process this new flow. Network applications, making use of the abstraction provided by the controller, could be configured to detect whenever a non-critical path is being traversed within the network because a malicious flow along that path would need to get requested from the controller. This can be done by creating a white list of critical paths, the application would check the path of the flow request against the white list and if it is not in the white list then that flow request can be determined to be suspicious/malicious because it is not making use of a network path that is critical to the functionality of the EPC.

The logical flow of the system is presented in Figure 1.3 and will be discussed from the bottom up. Firstly one of the OpenFlow enabled switches receives a data flow request that it can not process as it does not currently have that flow rule inside its flow table. The switch therefore reaches out to the controller with the flow request. The controller is configured to pass all flow requests onto the NIPS application. The NIPS checks the flow request's path against the white list of critical paths that were preconfigured. The NIPS would then be able to tell the difference between legitimate or suspicious flows within the EPC.

In addition to the ability of the SDN controller to distinguish malicious flows from critical ones, comes the ability to quarantine an infected node once it has been determined to be performing suspicious activities. The flow requests from the suspicious node could be rerouted to a decoy such that more information could be gathered on the attacker while not alerting the attacker. This information could be used by MNOs to create other systems that analyse inputs for patterns similar to the attackers.

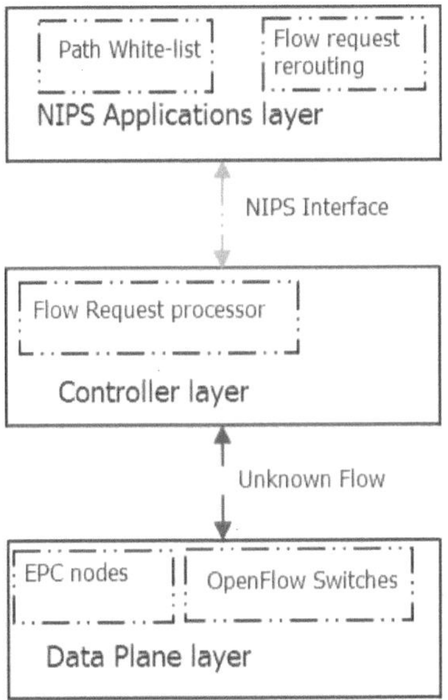



Figure 1.3: Simplified logical data flow between EPC entities, OpenFlow enabled switches, controller and the NIPS application

Network Functions Virtualisation (NFV) allows for virtual network functions to be programmatically deployable. These VNF's are the perfect candidate to be used as decoys as each of the entities inside the EPC have already been virtualised by previous research [15]. Only once an attack has been detected by the Network application, will the decoy need to get deployed. This ability for decoy VNFs to get programmatically deployed only when necessary will be a great benefit for MNOs as opposed to the alternative that involves permanently running a physical decoy machine.

In this book SDN and NFV are shown to be effective at defending the EPC from attackers internal to the EPC by automatically detecting flows that make use of non critical paths within the EPC. These flows would be detected as malicious, as there would be no other reason for them to get requested from the controller. Once a malicious flow is detected, the threat would autonomously get contained by leveraging the controller's ability to redirect flows. The flows from the compromised node would get redirected to a decoy version of its initial target, which is deployed programmatically by NFV techniques only once it is required. The system would also be capable of asynchronously alerting the MNO operatives about the attack so that they can respond accordingly while at the same time containing the attack.

## 1.1 Research Motivation

MNOs face a crisis of trust with their users [16]. Securing users' information as well as ensuring the continued functionality of their networks remains a high priority. MNOs are constantly trying to get better performance from their networks in order to entice more customers even though it is known that as the use of a network increases, so too does the probability of being targeted by malicious actors. The opportunity is available to leverage off new technologies, such as SDN and NFV, in order to apply new methods of securing the mobile core networks.

The main aim of SDN is to enable logically centralized control for the network by means of abstractions such as, allowing for a global network view and introducing a programmatic interface to the network switches. This allows for software defined rules to be put in place on a network in terms of flows between entities within the EPC.

One of the concerns with the EPC's security is that the basic entities required for the EPC to function are not secured against attackers that have infiltrated the same network that the entities reside on. Current IDSs are limited by the fact that they can not distinguish between flows that make use of critical and non critical paths within a network. So if attackers have achieved knowledge of the network layout without being detected (eg. insider information, or finding IP addresses of other nodes in configuration files or logs) then they would be able to laterally traverse through the network directly to other nodes.

In order to defend the EPC from internal attacks while not limiting its functionality, performance and the Quality of Service (QoS) offered to subscribers, strict control needs to be asserted over flows within the network. By utilising the global network view of the controller, paths between entities in the network that are critical to its functionality can be white listed such that network traffic flows are limited to those paths. If a switch requests a flow rule from the controller that makes use of a path that is not in the white list of critical paths then that flow can be marked as conspicuous and actions can be taken to mitigate the possible threat. The controller compares the source and destination of the request in order to determine what path is being traversed.

In non SDN enabled networks, the only response once a threat has been detected would be to drop the connections [17]. With SDN, network controlling applications are then able to automatically react to the alerts. MNOs would like to gather information on an attacker once they are detected in order to be able to best deal with the situation. It would also be preferential for the attacker to not realise that their actions have alerted the MNO of their presence so that more information can be gathered.

A decoy is designed to appear as a fully functioning network node but actually functions to obtain information on those that connect to it and convince the attacker that they are interacting with a legitimate node on the network. A controller is capable of altering any flow in the network by altering which network path the data flows along, therefore a compromised node can be contained by redirecting all network traffic flows attempting to make use of a non critical path to an HVA, directly to a decoy version of the HVA.

Figure 1.4 shows how this could be achieved, first the compromised node (red) makes an attempt to communicate with an HVA, that generates a malicious (red) flow which is requested from the controller. The controller and

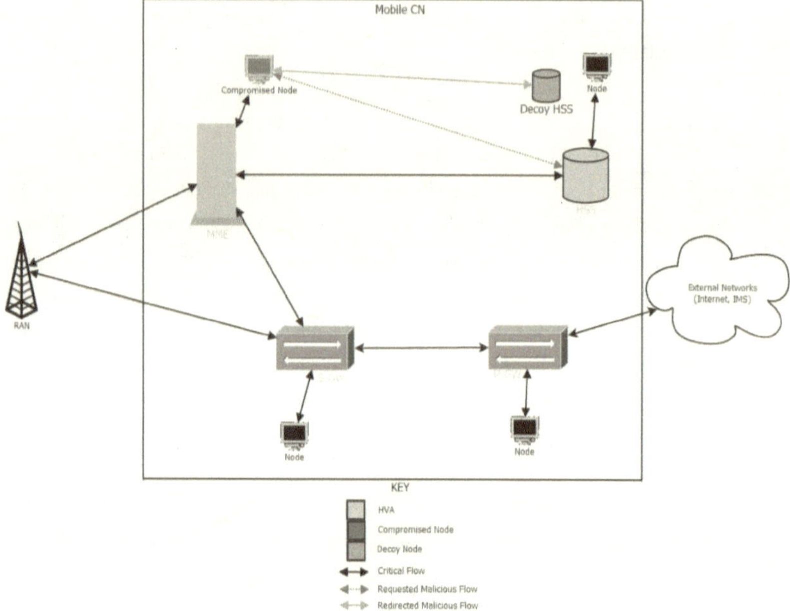



Figure 1.4: Malicious flow being redirected to a decoy version of its intended target

network applications are able to determine that the flow is not making use of a path in the white list of critical paths. This then triggers the controller to redirect flows originating from the compromised node to a decoy version of the intended target (green flow and node). The attacker would not be alerted that they have been detected as the decoy version would appear to them as the legitimate target, therefore ensuring the MNO operatives have time to react to the infiltration without the attacker causing any harm to the network or exfiltrating any valuable data. The HVA node would remain functioning as expected throughout this process.

MNOs would not like to waste their resources on having a decoy for each of their HVAs running at all times in case of an attack. Network Function

Virtualisation (NFV) allows for network functions of the EPC to be deployed as Virtual Network Functions (VNFs). Therefore by utilising NFV, the specific decoy of the attacker's intended target could be deployed only once it is necessary. The decoy would get deployed with dummy data which the attacker would find indistinguishable from the real data residing on the HVA. The network application (seen in Figure 1.3) that detects the malicious flow would be able to programmatically deploy a specific VNF based upon the attackers intended target.

SDN is used in this research to make use of the network controller's ability to have a holistic view of flows within the network [18, 19] and allowing for the differentiation between critical and non critical paths within the EPC. SDN also allows for a programmatic way in which to react to flows that request to make use of non critical paths. A network application could therefore get alerted to the malicious flow and then logically quarantine the compromised node by redirecting flows towards decoy version of the intended target. NFV is essential to this research as it allows for the automated configuration and implementation of a decoy HVA on the network as a VNF only once an attack has been detected.

In the worst case scenario, which involves an attacker having the foresight to traverse only the critical paths to get to an HVA, this system would not get triggered. This research still drastically lowers the paths that an attacker would be able follow in order to target an HVA. This small set of paths could then have higher levels of monitoring applied to them to detect malicious behaviours.

## 1.1.1 Problem Definition

Research on securing a EPC has mainly been focussed on the perimeter defences of the network, therefore, if an attacker successfully bypasses these defenses they can achieve a foothold in the network. From the initial foothold, the attacker could lay dormant within the EPC for large amounts of time, gathering up information at the same time [20]. The attacker would also be able to spread to other nodes throughout the EPC as all lateral movements throughout the EPC are deemed to be trusted. Attackers generally make use of an island hopping attack once they have infiltrated a network, which involves laterally moving between network nodes, beginning at their entry point and moving towards an HVA [21]. MNOs would want security measures deployed that would alert them as timeously as possible to mitigate any malicious activities being performed within their EPC.

As MNOs are advancing towards 5G, the mobile EPC is heading towards being virtualised through the use of SDN and NFV techniques, this presents a chance to leverage these paradigms in order to develop new techniques for increasing security around the EPC entities. The specific security issue covered is to reduce the number of paths that attackers would be able to traverse while laterally moving between network entities within an EPC that the attacker has compromised.

Security measures put in place must not hinder the overall functionality of the EPC because that would lead to the measures never being implemented; there must always be a balance between security and usability/functionality of a system that is open to such large volumes of traffic.

Differentiating between flows over critical and non critical paths does not keep attackers out but is able to limit and constrain lateral movement between the nodes of the EPC by only allowing for critical network pathways to be followed.

EPC elements are designed to have quick responses to valid communications. If an attacker were to find themselves on a compromised node inside the EPC, they would be able to exploit this open level of trust that entities have within the EPC. The attacker would be able to mimic the expected signals as the communication standards that the EPC entities rely on are public knowledge.

The network application needs to automatically contain the attack by deploying a virtualised version of the intended target which the attacker would then get redirected to. This is in order to convince the attacker they are being successful in their attack while gathering intelligence on the attacker.

This work also needs to include a comprehensive literature review on other research performed on the threats presented to the EPC. The literature review will need to detail how SDN and NFV have been utilised to improve upon the security of other networks.

The primary goal of this research is the design and implementation of a SDN based EPC that utilises a network application to detect malicious network flows. These malicious flows are assumed to be instigated by an attacker while attempting lateral movement within the EPC. This work will include how the application will respond to a detected malicious behaviour in order to mitigate the threat.

### 1.1.2   Research Questions

The main questions to be investigated by this research are as follows:

- Can the use of SDN and NFV on a mobile EPC lead to better security for the critical EPC entities.

- Would a SDN based NIPS be able to warn MNOs of an attacker within their EPC while also automatically quarantining the attacker to mitigate damages or data leaks.

- If strict flow rules are applied on an EPC such that only flows which make use of critical network paths are allowed, would this hinder the functionality of the EPC.

- Will an intruder be detected due to the irregularities of their actions on the network.

- Is a network application capable of detecting malicious activity in the network and consequently reacting to this detection in order prevent the attacker from causing damage to, effecting the functionality of, or extracting data from the EPC.

- Would the automated quarantining of the compromised node alert the attacker to their detection.

## 1.2   Scope and Limitations

The scope of this research is limited to the benefits of using SDN and NFV techniques in order to secure an EPC from internal attacks. Other security aspects pertaining to Long Term Evolution (LTE) and the EPC specifically are out of scope and were only visited and discussed in the literature review.

The scope is further limited to defending from an attacker that has already achieved control over a node within the EPC. The attacker is presumed to have full admin rights on the entry node (root privileges assuming a Unix node).

The EPC is limited to being only made up of the essential entities, comprised of Home Subscriber Server (HSS), Packet Data Network Gateway (P-GW), Serving Gateway (S-GW) and Mobility Management Entity (MME). Other add on modules are not considered in this research.

The scope is also limited to the specific example of an attacker having compromised an administration node (jump box) and is directly targeting the HSS of the EPC.

## 1.3   The book Structure

The following sections summarise the content of each chapter of the book as well as provide an overview of the book.

### 1.3.1 A Review of EPC Security as well as Techniques Utilising SDN and NFV in Order to Secure Networks (Chapter 2)

This chapter provides a brief background on the EPC as well as an overview of the current LTE EPC standard and the security architecture and attack vectors associated with it. This chapter also reviews other research that has been presented in terms of security functionalities that have been implemented with the SDN and NFV paradigms.

### 1.3.2 Requirements and Design of NIPS for the EPC (Chapter 3)

This chapter presents the requirements for the proposed NIPS, based on typical patterns deployed by attackers within a network. The logic of the SDN network application is designed including the programmatic steps that will be followed. The overall architecture of the proposed solution is finally decided upon at the end of this chapter.

### 1.3.3 Implementation of the Security Architecture (Chapter 4)

This chapter presents the implementation of the EPC with our designed security architecture as well as how this system was deployed for evaluation purposes. The methods by which internal attackers are detected and systematically responded to is presented.

### 1.3.4 Results and Analysis (Chapter 5)

This chapter presents the results of our implementation of an EPC that utilises SDN control plane applications to control, detect and respond to internal attackers by deploying virtualised versions of the attacks target. The information gathered on the attacker is also presented and analysis is performed as to how effectively the information can be acted upon.

### 1.3.5 Conclusion (Chapter 6)

The **book** is concluded in this chapter along with proposing future work
that can be performed in this area of research.

# Chapter 2

# BACKGROUND AND LITERATURE SURVEY

The previous section introduced the basic concepts and aims of this research, including the security concerns around the EPC [22]. This section first gives a brief background on the EPC architecture and then presents a more in depth review of some of the most prevalent security concerns the EPC faces. The previous section also introduced SDN and NFV technologies and how their implementation in an EPC architecture can potentially be utilised to mitigate a specific security concern of the EPC. The following section provides more background on those paradigms and also covers how research has been performed using these technologies to improve network security.

## 2.1 Evolved Packet Core Architecture

The EPC is the technical name for the Core Network of the Third Generation Partnership Project's (3GPP) Long Term Evolution (LTE) system. The LTE system provides great improvements on both the Radio Access side as well as the packet core side when compared to legacy mobile systems such as 2G, GSM and CDMA. The EPC allows for backwards compatibility to legacy technologies allowing for a convergence of mobile networks [23]. 4G/LTE has been designed as an All-IP architecture and has replaced the hybrid Circuit Switched (CS) and Packet Switched (PS) domain that was inherited from 2G/3G with a pure PS EPC.

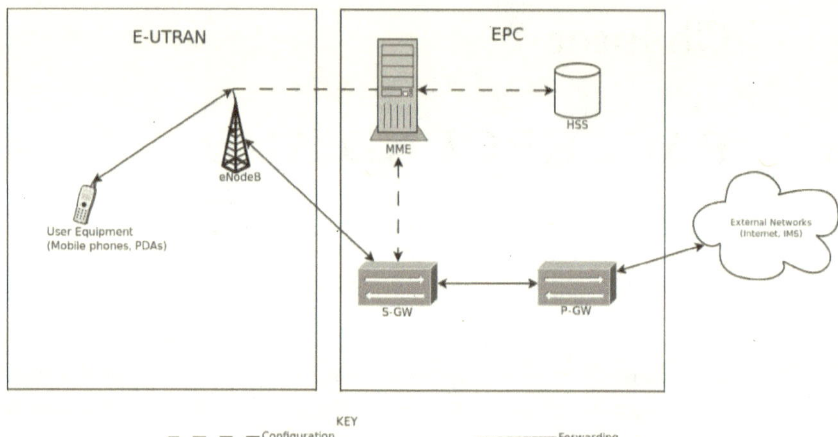


Figure 2.1: Fundamental components that make up the 4G architecture

The overall 4G architecture in Figure 2.1 is separated into two parts. Firstly, the Evolved Universal Terrestrial Radio Access Network (E-UTRAN) which focusses on the base station and radio access to the network, and secondly the EPC which is comprised of several key components which are broken down as follows:

- The Packet Data Network Gateway (P-GW) is the contact point of the EPC to external networks such as the Internet or IP Multimedia System (IMS). The P-GW also assigns User Equipment (UE) an IP[4].

- The Serving Gateway (S-GW), which behaves as an entry point for the UE into the Core Network (CN) from the RAN, as well as gathering information on sessions for billing purposes.

- The Home Subscriber Server (HSS) contains a database of all users' subscription information and is responsible for determining what level of QoS a user is allowed on the network. The HSS also performs authentication and authorization of the user.

- The Mobility Management Entity (MME) is in charge of signal processing between the EPC and the UE. The MME is responsible for initially setting up the control of sessions by authenticating the user with the HSS. Once a session is authenticated, the MME determines which S-GW to anchor the UE to. The MME is also responsible for detecting that a UE has changed coverage areas and therefore migrates an existing session to a different S-GW.

### 2.1.1 Vulnerabilities and Security concerns in the EPC

Vulnerabilities within Mobile Networks (MN) can be defined as weaknesses in any component present in the overall architecture of the system. These weaknesses are then able to be exploited in order for an attack on the MN to be conducted.

No research could be found that explicitly looks at defending an EPC from an attack that has already successfully gained internal access to the EPC. Research focus has been primarily on the perimeter defences of the EPC, and effectively relying on the design of the EPC to keep it secure by use of communication protocols between nodes that ensure Authentication, Authorisation, and Accounting (AAA) such as the DIAMETER protocol [24]. This is an important gap in current research because once an attacker has compromised a node within the EPC, and were given free reign to laterally move throughout the network to HVAs, they would be able to perform any of the following attacks [25, 26] :

- Intellectual property theft

- Information technology sabotage

- Unauthorised data extraction

- Corporate espionage

- Data tampering

- Asset destruction

- Installing malicious software on other nodes.

- Resource misuse (eg. crytocurrency mining)

- Social engineering on MNO clients

- Fraud with MNOs customers banking details

- Spoofing

- Eavesdropping

Paolini et al states that the decision to transfer to a flat IP architecture has caused a shift in mobile wireless entry points [27]. The transfer to an all IP based network has opened up the mobile EPC to all the vulnerabilities associated with other traditional IP networks such as the Internet [28].

Modern MNOs rely mostly on perimeter security mechanisms mostly based on the understanding that the edges of the network are the most vulnerable to attacks stemming from external sources. The edge of MNs are heavily protected with firewalls, IPSs, Network Address Translators (NATs) and Customer Edge Switching (CES). The heavy focus on MN edge protection has led to the internal network being open to attacks on unaddressed vulnerabilities [28].

The EPC makes use of the GPRS Tunnelling Protocol (GTP) to manage mobility and QoS functionality [22]. Park et al. covered several security issues stemming from the use of the GPRS Tunnelling Protocol (GTP) and are presented as follows[29]:

- The work from Park et al. presents a scanning attack where an attacker could use GTP echo messages to scan the layout and other information relating to the targeted EPC. This info leak could then act as an initial reconnaissance for later escalation of attacks

- It is also shown in the work from Park et al. that a possible resource exhaustion attack could be conducted to exhaust the resources of a P-GW by sending through a flood of Create Session GTP messages.

- Create Session messages are shown to also be able to target individual users on the MNO network by sending said create message with a falsified number of a targeted user. This user would not be able to utilise the mobile network.

- GTP fuzzing is shown to be able to interrupt the functionality of an EPC entity. Fuzzing by means of malformed GTP packets could cause systems to malfunction when receiving said packets. Fuzzing is shown to be a legitimate attack due to the backwards compatibility of the 4G EPC, essentially allowing for a downgrade attack.

The four elements of the EPC presented in 2.1 are critical to its functionality. Attacks on, or compromisation of these entities could result in the following:

- If the contents of an HSS were to be leaked then the authenticity, integrity and confidentiality of all connections to the MNO would be compromised.

- If either of the gateways (S-GW or P-GW) are compromised then the attacker would be able to perform Man in the Middle (MITM) attacks as well as rerouteing all traffic to illicit sources.

- If the MME were to be hindered then all users would be unable to connect with new sessions to the network as well as not being able to change coverage areas, rendering the entire system unusable.

### 2.1.2   Research into securing the EPC

Quang et al claims that once a component in the EPC gets compromised, the attacker would be able to traverse through the network; their proposed mitigation is a DIAMETER based security framework [30]. DIAMETER is an

Authorization, Authentication and Accounting (AAA) protocol that is used within the EPC as an update of the RADIUS protocol, it offers enhancements such as Transport Layer Security (TLS) compatibility and, because it is TCP based as opposed to UDP based it is seen as being more reliable.

NEMESYS presents research into predicting abnormal behaviour from mobile users by monitoring the control plane and billing data [31]. NEMESYS also makes use of honeypots/decoys in their research although they simulate UE as their honeypots in order to entice mobile malware to connect to them such that analysis can be performed on the malware to further improve on the detection capabilities of the NEMESYS system. NEMESYS is more targeted at the security of the mobile devices that are connected to the mobile network.

ASMONIA takes a thorough accounting of the threats and risks associated with mobile terminals and communication networks [32]. ASMONIA is also targeted mostly at the security of the UE connected to the EPC. The system analyses traffic going through the EPC for malicious patterns or signatures such that further action can be taken.

## 2.2 Software-Defined Networking and Network Functions Virtualisation

Two of the paradigms that MNOs are switching to and applying to the EPC are Software Defined Networks (SDN) and Network Functions Virtualisation (NFV). Both SDN and NFV are slated as being the next big changes in the telecommunications industry due to them addressing the challenges that have been most pertinent in next generation networks such as the 3GPP's 5G specification, and both are receiving extensive research in order to be applied to the new 5G standard [15]. When SDN and NFV are utilised, networks are able to become more agile and are able to transform the topology and

functionality of the network in an automated fashion in order to scale on
demand [33, 34].

## 2.2.1   SDN architecture

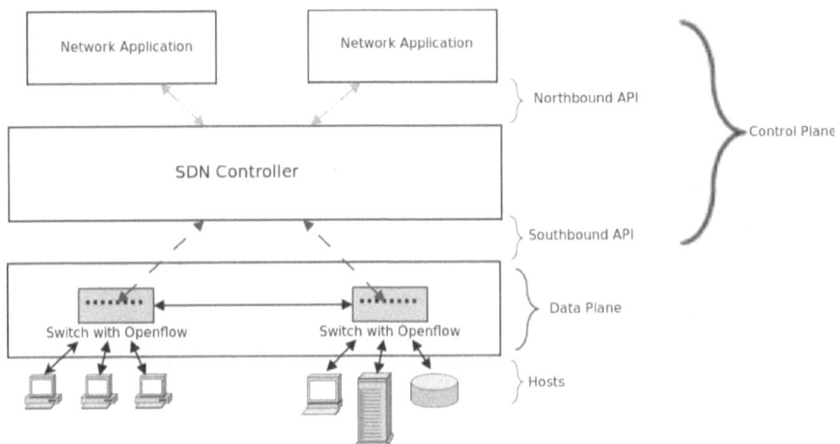


Figure 2.2: SDN architecture

SDN allows for the separation of data and control planes. This allows
for a logically centralized controller that can then have a holistic view of the
network as each node reports with its state back to the controller [35]. SDN
allows for control functions to run as network applications within the logically
centralised controller. Another common term for SDN controller is the Network Operating System (NOS). The controller provides network applications
with a global network view as well as a programmatic interface (Northbound
API) for manipulation of the network's forwarding devices (Data Plane) [14].

This architecture of separation of control from data planes, allows for the
switches in a network to be simpler devices with limited logic built into them,
switches can be reduced to basic packet forwarding devices containing flow

24

tables populated with flows specified by the controller. The flow rules describe how incoming packets get handled based on the matching fields (such as packet header content, source/destination address/port, etc.). The key enabler for this functionality is the OpenFlow (Southbound API) protocol which allows for the controller to communicate with switches. With the SDN controller being logically centralised, this allows for the controller to be hosted on general purpose servers [36].

The full technical architectural background of SDN can be found in Appendix A.

### 2.2.2   NFV Background

NFV is the second of the new paradigms that MNOs are switching to and applying to the EPC. NFV is a framework that allows for network functions to be separated from proprietary hardware appliances and enables dynamic methods to construct and manage network functions with virtualisation techniques. Modern virtualisation platforms are able to be utilised as well as commercial off the shelf hardware in order to deploy the functionalities required for telecommunications networks [37]. A more detailed technical breakdown of NFV can be found in Appendix B.

## 2.3   Use of SDN and NFV in security

SDN is able to enhance network security for two reasons, first is the centralisation of the network control plane which allows for the global visibility of the behaviour of network traffic as well as the holistic state of the network. Second, is the programmability achievable on data forwarding elements that comes as part of SDN. Together it is now possible to have instantaneous threat mitigation and automated responses due to the runtime network monitoring, as well as simplifying the configuration and adjustments of security policies in one centralised location instead of individual device alterations within the network [38].

An SDN based network security system for defence against Distributed
Denial of Service (DDoS) attacks was patented by Han et al., their system
involved an IDS that would sample network traffic and devise an action plan
as to how to react to the threat, this action plan would then get passed to
the network controller for analysis; the patent does not explicitly state what
actions the controller performs [39].

Using SDN to improve on the security of the EPC has been proposed
before by Kempf et al. [22]. Kempf et al. put forward a means to isolate
the mobile equipment once the terminal has been identified as being high
risk. It proposes rerouting all traffic from the infected terminal to a logically
separated network where malware gets removed from the device, only once
the terminal is deemed healthy is the terminal allowed back onto the EPC.
Their research does not cover the case for when the attacker has already
penetrated into the EPC.

"Detection as a service" (DaaS) presents a cloud based service that monitors traffic through the gateways of an EPC. The service involves an IDS
that is deployed at the networks gateways and utilises the controller to block
detected malicious flows [40]. A similar approach is presented in this work
with the difference being that DaaS monitors the flows from the subscribers
of the MN, therefore leaving the flows throughout the internals of the EPC
unmonitored and allowing for internal attackers to traverse the network at
will. The work in this book ensures that internal flows are monitored.

Lin et al. researched modifying the SDN architecture with NFV in order
to deploy an IPS as a VNF in the data plane [41]. Their study mostly focussed on limiting the traffic overhead faced by the controller and the service
chaining problem. The service chaining problem being the technical difficul-
ties associated with how best to order network services (such as firewalls and
network address translation) when adding to a network system that already
is compromised of many different network services.

Virtual Network Security Functions (vNSF) are presented in work by Battula et al., the vNSFs are utilised to ensure End to End (E2E) security within a data centre [42]. The presented vNSFs include a Firewall (FW), IPSec and an IPS which is utilised to perform Deep Packet Inspection (DPI) and signature recognition.

A survey on the interfaces used by NFV security services is performed in [43]. The survey covers security applications that require IPS, honeypots, DPI, FW and Virtual Private Networks (VPN). The survey presents the required security applications within a MN include security requests from UE, negotiation of security functions and security around the configuration of the network, the latter is important to this research.

Monshizadeh et al. presents an analysis on the security concepts of the Open Platform for NFV (OPNFV) and presents their findings as to how a telecommunications as a service can be created that makes use of SDN and NFV to allow for Mobile Virtual Network Operators (MVNOs) to securely share resources [44]. This work is more focussed on the general security concerns that have arisen around the SDN and NFV paradigms themselves.

Software Defined Mobile Networks (SDMN) and the security aspects pertaining to SDMNs are presented in works of Liyanage et al [38, 45]. SDMNs are considered to be MNs that make use of cloud computing, NFV and SDN. Liyanage et al. present a multi tiered approach to secure both the SDMN subscribers as well as the network itself. The original work by Liyanage et al. presents a technique to secure the communication channels within the SDMN by leveraging on the Host Identity Protocol (HIP) and IPSec [45]. Restrictions to the back haul network are also installed by use of policy based communication which in turn is shown to prevent source address spoofing and DoS attacks. In a follow up paper, Liyanage et al. presents further research into the security of SDMNs, with the introduction of Software Defined Monitoring (SDM) to orchestrate the functionalities previously presented as well as a DPI technique to target specific malicious detected flows [38]. The main takeaway from the research into SDMNs is the fact that it is possible to automate mitigation and reactionary procedures within a SDN and NFV enabled network by setting up rules within the controller to provide countermeasures and mitigation actions. Liyanage et al. also validates that a combination of sources of information on an SDMN can lead to accurate and rapid detection of attacks to the network [38]. This research lacks the focus on protecting the individual EPC entities in the case of a compromised element within the EPC.

## 2.4   Chapter Discussions

This chapter first presented an overview of the EPC architecture, as well as presenting some of the security concerns raised on this architecture. Secondly SDN and NFV architectures were discussed with a focus on the ability of applications within the control plane to mitigate malicious flows by modifying their flow destination. Evidence to support this was provided through a thorough review of relevant literature within this research area. Many current security solutions for MNs utilising SDN and NFV techniques focus on the subscriber security and continue the pattern of focussing protection for the EPC on the edges on the network. From the literature review it is evident that the HVAs of the EPC have not been considered to be attacked by compromised nodes within the same LAN segment, therefore allowing for an attacker to traverse through the EPC without being detected.

The following chapter will present the requirements of an SDN based system to protect the HVAs of an EPC, as well as providing the design of the proposed solution.

# Chapter 3

# Requirements and Design of NIPS for the EPC

The previous section presented the existing work on using SDN and NFV to improve on network security as well as highlighting the fact that currently there is not any research into securing the EPC from attacks that have achieved a foothold in the internals of the EPC. No research was identified that secures the internals of the EPC. The main aim of this **book** is to provide a solution that will defend the EPC from attackers that have already compromised a node within the network, this will be done by lever-aging SDN and NFV techniques. This section will look at the requirements of the proposed NIPS based on typical attacker behaviours. From this, the algorithm used for the logic of the NIPS will be presented as well as the architecture for the proposed system.

## 3.1 NIPS requirements

MNOs would never implement a security feature onto their EPC that compromises the base functionality of their EPC. Therefore maintaining the overall functionality of the EPC highly influences the design and requirements for this research. SDN and NFV are beneficial to the specific problem of attackers already compromising a node in the EPC because of SDN's ability to monitor and orchestrate all of the traffic within a network without diminishing EPC performance, whereas NFV allows for specific and flexible VNFs to be deployed to draw malicious users away from the EPC that will still be running as intended.

### 3.1.1 General attacker patterns

The NIPS needs to be able to mitigate the typical patterns that are followed by attackers. An attacker is what modern media portrays as a hacker. Attackers are users that have malicious intent with their target system. The following section details some of the typical patterns followed by attackers in order to justify the requirements for the NIPS and are based off the work in [46].

Initially an attacker would compromise a node within the network by exploiting a vulnerability within the network (a list of vulnerabilities associated with an EPC is available in List 1.1). Once an attacker has achieved a foot-hold in the EPC, they would then be ignorant to the topology of the EPC. The attacker needs to become better informed about the layout of the network. In order to do this, a reconnaissance attack would be performed. This attack has multiple variances including mapping every reachable node in the network from the compromised node (also known as the entry point). This is facilitated in part by IP and DNS scanning techniques. The major goals of an attackers reconnaissance attacks are two fold: [21]

First is to collect technical details about the systems corresponding to each network node reachable from the entry point. This includes comparing signatures for operating systems as well as their configuration. Traffic flows from the compromised node are also sniffed to garner more information about the network. This information can give the attacker a better idea of how to compromise the other nodes in the network.

Second goal is to map the network topology. This is usually achieved by means of a graph search strategy of all nodes contactable from the entry point. This can give the attacker a better understanding of how to traverse the network towards their intended target/s.

Attackers could also get more details about other nodes in the network by searching through the application configurations or logs of the entry node. In this case the reconnaissance would not make any network calls. In this situation the attacker would not need to perform a full network scan which is beneficial to the attacker as full network scans are considered noisy and attract attention.

Once the attacker has performed reconnaissance on the other nodes in the network, the attacker would then be able to perform further attacks on the other identified nodes within the network. Attackers would next target HVAs which were identified, because the HVAs would provide the attacker with the most prominent gain for all their previously expended effort and being able to query or corrupt an HVA would be the attackers end goal. Further attacks could come in the following forms:

- Undetected intrusion attacks such as modifying, monitoring or running software implementations on any of the nodes [47].

- Data exfiltration from a HVA such as a main database (ie. HSS for the case of the EPC).

- Bringing down the HVA by means of crippling its underlying infrastructure or flooding the HVA with malformed messages [48].

The best defence for any network would be to remove all vulnerabilities from their networks therefore denying any attacker a starting point for the overall attack playbook. But the total elimination of vulnerabilities from any wide reaching system such as the EPC seems to be an ever lasting endeavour and new vulnerabilities are constantly being identified by researchers [21].

### 3.1.2 Requirements

Based on the typical behaviours exhibited by an attacker described above, we can determine the following requirements for a NIPS that mitigates attacks on the EPC:

- Minimise the paths that an attacker can traverse without being detected, because comprehensive reconnaissance makes use of every network path available to the compromised node. This minimisation of legitimate network paths to traverse, increases the probability of an attacker attempting to make use of a path that would trigger an alert whenever attempting a lateral movement within the network.

- Ability to discern between network flows that make use of critical and non critical network paths. This distinction will allow for automated detection and responses whenever a non critical path is attempted to be traversed. While also allowing for all legitimate flows that are experienced within a functioning EPC to continue functioning correctly.

- Detection of flows that are making use of non critical paths. An EPC that is functioning as expected will never make use of a non critical network path, therefore it is assumed that data attempting to flow across a non critical path has malicious intent. MNO operatives need to be alerted to this malicious activity within their EPC.

- Containment of the compromised node that instigated the detected malicious flow. This will prevent the attacker from causing further harm to the EPC while the MNO operatives are able to act on mitigating the overall attack.

- Respond to the overall attack by alerting the MNO operatives as well as quarantining the compromised node in an automated fashion.

- Do not tip off the attacker that their actions have triggered a warning, effectively stalling the attacker such that the MNO operatives have time to act accordingly.

## 3.2 Design of SDN NIPS application algorithm

The first design decision that needs to be made is how to ensure that our NIPS does not interfere with the base functionality of an EPC. Given that there are only a handful of critical network paths between entities in a typical EPC set-up, it is entirely feasible to initially configure the NIPS system with a white-list of allowed network paths that are critical to the EPC's functionality. Any data flows across those white-listed network paths will not be affected by the proposed NIPS, therefore ensuring the functionality of the EPC remains unaffected.

The second design decision was how to detect an attacker within the network. Based on the white-list of allowed network paths an SDN application could be written to determine whenever a network path is being requested that is not within the white list of allowed network paths. Every network request made within a network will be monitored by the logically centralised controller utilising SDN, therefore logic can be implemented within the control plane that can distinguish between critical and non critical flows throughout the EPC based on the pre-configured white list of network paths.

After an attack has been detected, it has been stated that the attack should get contained. With the use of an SDN enabled network, flows can get redirected, therefore once a node has been identified as the source of a malicious network path request, the SDN application will be capable of re-routing all future malicious requests from the compromised node away from their intended targets. Only once the attacker instigates an attempt at laterally moving to specific HVA does the decoy for the HVA get deployed.

The NIPS application needs to trigger a response to the attack. It was determined that two parallel automated responses should take place once the attack is detected. The first of these responses would be to send out an alert to the MNO operatives that are responsible for the maintenance and overall operations of the EPC. The other response goes hand in hand with the containment steps above. Once the attack is detected a decoy VNF version of the intended target should get deployed. The SDN application would then be able to re-route all network flows that were originally aimed at the HVA towards the decoy version. This would cause the attacker to think that they have been successful in their attempt at lateral movement from their entry point towards their targeted HVA. This would therefore delay the attacker, as they attempt more malicious activities on the decoy, such that the alerted MNO operatives can act further to stop the attack.

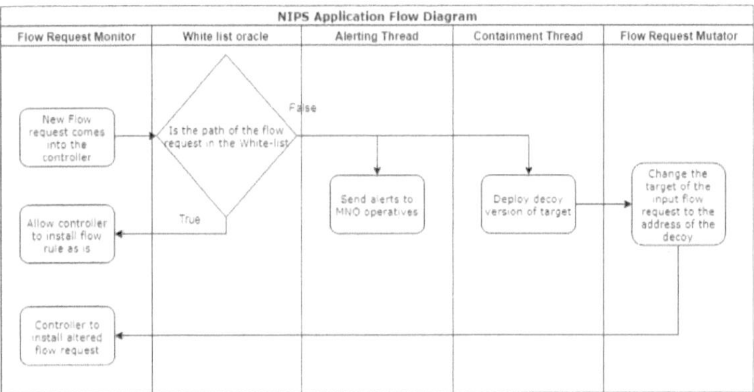



Figure 3.1: Flow diagram for the logic in the NIPS application

The overall logical decisions and processes of the SDN NIPS application can be found in Figure 3.1 and Algorithm 1. Step 1 is triggered whenever a switch in the network receives a flow request that it does not already have a flow table entry for, the switch then contacts the controller with the flow request which is processed by the controller and triggers off the NIPS functionality.

---

**Algorithm 1** NIPS application

---

 1: new flow request $Fr$ made of controller
 2: set $Wl$ as the list of critical network paths
 3: set $P$ as the path required for flow ($P \leftarrow Fr.path$)
 4: **if** $P$ is in $Wl$ **then**
 5:     update switches with valid $Fr$
 6: **else**
 7:     send alerts
 8:     $HVAtype \leftarrow Fr.destination.nodetype$
 9:     deploy decoy $D$ of type $HVAtype$
10:     alter $Fr$ by replacing the *destination* field with $D$'s address
11:     update switches with mutated $Fr'$

---

The flow request that is received at the controller will have all the properties of the requested flow such as the source and destination nodes of the flow, which is the same as knowing the path that the flow will be making use of. Configuration will also be managed such that the node type is known for all nodes in the network.

The conditional logic (oracle function) in step 4 is to determine whether the incoming flow request is malicious or not. Step 5 is a simple case that allows the controller to process the requested flow as it is, this is for the non malicious flow case which is what would be the most common occurrence within a normally operating EPC. The overhead incurred to get to Step 5 is kept at a minimal in order to prevent any extra latency within the regularly functioning EPC.

Steps 7 though 11 cover the case of a flow request being identified as malicious. In this case fast containment, alerting and response times are essential. Therefore two parallel/asynchronous process streams will get triggered. First is to send the alerts out to the MNO operatives, step 7 gets executed in parallel with the steps 8 to 11. The other parallel stream involves identifying what type of decoy to deploy based on the node type of the destination of the flow request (ie steps 8 and 9). The final steps (10 and 11) of this second stream is to alter the malicious flow request to change the destination to the newly deployed decoy. This is done by altering the flow request by replacing the original flow requests destination address field with the destination address of the newly deployed decoy. The decoy is configured to behave exactly the same as the HVA node that it is mimicking. The mutated flow request is then processed by the controller therefore redirecting the compromised node's data flows to the decoy node. Thus ensuring that all malicious traffic originating from the compromised node goes towards the decoy and the EPC is able to continue functioning correctly. The delay between the start of step 8 to the end of step 11 needs to be short enough that the attacker is not alerted to the processes, this time is subjective depending on the geographic dispersion of the network elements as this affects response times between network nodes without and NIPS triggering processes.

## 3.3 Functional Architecture of the NIPS

With the NIPS applications' logical design described it is now possible to discuss the entire systems architecture that is presented in Figure 3.2. The system consists of three layers based on the SDN paradigm. The applications layer, the controller layer and the data plan layer. The functions of each layer will now be described in a top down approach.

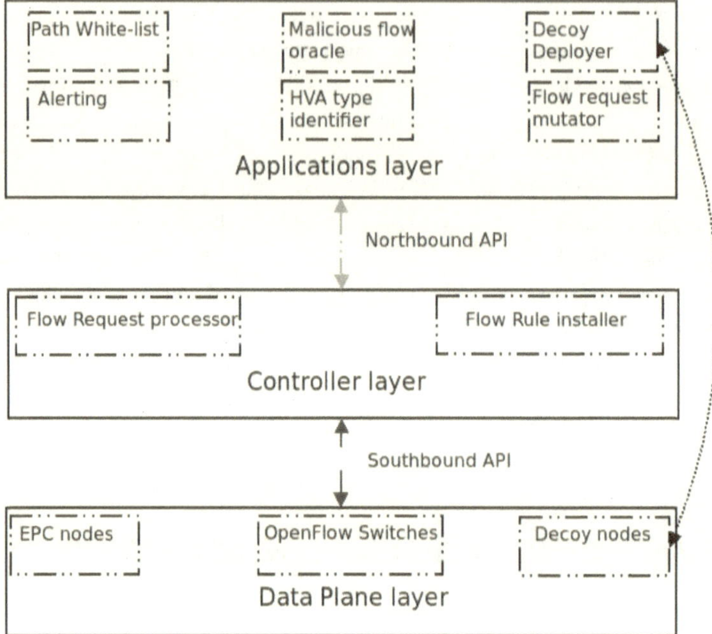


Figure 3.2: Functional architecture of proposed NIPS

The application layer consists of a white list of critical network paths. All
flow requests get their path checked against the white list by the malicious
flow oracle function. The alerting system that gets triggered in the case of a
malicious flow resides in the application layer. Determining the type of decoy
needed along with the functionality to deploy decoy nodes are contained in
the application level. A flow request mutator is also implemented at application level.

The controller layer is preconfigured in a way that whenever a new flow
request is made of it, it does not process it straight away, it passes the flow
request onto the application layer. Only once the application layer replies
back with the flow request, does the controller process the flow request to

37

install a flow rule onto the data forwarding devices.

The data layer consists of all the nodes within the EPC, along with the switches that are used to connect the nodes together. The switches need to be compatible with a protocol that allows them to communicate with the controller. When a decoy node gets deployed it will reside in this layer as well.

The logical flow between the layers when reacting to an attacker is as such: The compromised node attempts to connect to an HVA within the EPC. The switch receives this network connection attempt but the switch does not recognise the path that has been requested as it is not contained in the switch's current flow table. The switch makes use of the Southbound API to make a flow request from the controller.

The controller receives the new flow request, which it is preconfigured to pass onto the application layer via the Northbound API. The NIPS application then checks whether the flow request is malicious or not, in the case of a legitimate flow request then the application passes the flow request back to the controller for processing.

In the case of the application determining that the flow request is malicious, firstly the alerting system is triggered. While asynchronously a decoy node gets deployed, once the decoy node has been provisioned, the flow request is altered to have the decoy as its destination. The mutated flow request is then passed back to the controller for processing.

Both legitimate and mutated flow requests get processed at the controller layer. The controller then replies back to the switch that instigated the flow request with a flow rule that it should implement for the rest of the packets in the instigating data flow.

## 3.4　Chapter Discussions

This chapter presented the requirements, design and general architecture for the proposed system. The requirements were decided upon based on the need for the system to not be detrimental to the EPC functionality as well as being able to mitigate typical patterns followed by attackers. From these requirements a design for the logic of the NIPS application was presented. Finally the overall architecture of the system was presented with a detailed description of the interactions between separate logical functions.

The following chapter will establish how the Proof of Concept (PoC) framework was created for this research system. Including a description of creating and deploying the NIPS network application and illustrating how it would effectively mitigate malicious users from laterally moving throughout the EPC.

# Chapter 4

# IMPLEMENTATION OF SDN BASED NIPS FOR THE EPC

The previous chapter presented the requirements for a NIPS to prevent attackers from laterally moving among entities in the EPC via non critical paths. The overall algorithm for the NIPS application was also presented, as well as a high level architecture detailing the interactions between the logical functions necessary for this system. This section describes how the proposed NIPS was implemented. A bottom up approach is followed based on Figure 3.2 describing how each layer of the SDN architecture was implemented as well as how the functions within those layers assist with the NIPS application. Finally the configuration and setup of the system for testing and evaluation purposes will be discussed.

## 4.1 Network Layer

Figure 3.2 shows the three components in the data plane, i.e., the EPC entities, the OpenFlow enabled switches and the decoy EPC nodes. A closer look at the specifics of the switches used in the network is presented first, followed by the overall network setup to enable the EPC's functionality.

### 4.1.1 OpenFlow Switches

OpenFlow switches come in both software and hardware form. Software switches were chosen for this research as they are more easily deployed while still allowing for the same interactions with the controller and not hindering any of the network application logic.

Open vSwitch (OVS) was the software switch selected because of its wide adoption and documentation as well as support for multiple OpenFlow versions [49]. OpenFlow version 1.3 was adopted as the Southbound interface between the switches and the SDN controller.

### 4.1.2 EPC Entities and Decoys

The OpenEPC is an implementation of the LTE EPC created by Core Network Dynamics [50]. The OpenEPC project virtualised the EPC using NFV techniques and allows for each EPC entity to be deployed as a single VNF. There are two main approaches to the implementation of VNFs, first is to have a dedicated VM for each specific VNF. The other way to implement VNFs is to use containerisation, which creates a dedicated container for individual VNFs. A full technical description of the differences between VMs and containers is presented in Appendix C.

The work presented by Fontenla et al. details how the OpenEPC was reworked into individual containers for each VNF required for an EPC [51]. The four basic functional nodes of the EPC were each implemented as individual containers i.e., HSS, MME, SGW and PGW. The container versions of the EPC entities were shown in Table C.1 to be more efficient in terms of both memory usage while running as well as storage of the VNFs. Therefore containerised VNFs were chosen due to their lower usage of computing resources.

In terms of the decoy VNFs to be deployed in the Network layer, containers have the advantage of being able to be spun up and be readily available for usage a lot faster than VMs [52]. The chances of deceiving the attacker that their lateral movement was successful are improved the faster the decoy can be deployed. This further cemented the choice to use the containerised VNFs from the OpenEPC. This is due to the fact that the included overhead would seem like typical network latency if the overhead is low enough. The container approach combined both the S-GW and the P-GW into one container which is referred to as the SPGW henceforth.

### 4.1.3 Network Environment

A network emulator was also required to run the SDN enabled EPC. Containernet, which is a mininet fork that allows for containers as hosts, was decided upon [53]. Containernet is a programmatic network emulator that allows for a number of virtual switches as well as virtual links between the container hosts and the switches to be created within a single Linux VM.

Containernet is a network orchestrator that utilises a Python API to programmatically define a network topology. OVS instances are used by Containernet for the software switches. The network links between container hosts and the switches are implemented using virtual Ethernet links. The OVS elements are each able to connect directly to a separate network controller. The Docker container platform is then used to deploy the container hosts. Containernet was chosen due to the low barrier to entry to get a PoC up and running as well as being a modern implementation of the popular Mininet project. A full technical breakdown of Containernet is presented in Appendix D.

A personal computer with 16 GB of RAM and a 3.2 GHz Intel i7 processor running an Ubuntu 18.04 Operating System (OS) was used as the base platform to host the virtual machine resources required for the Containernet environment. This was done to ensure that the NIPS and network environment was never constrained by physical computational resources during evaluation. The full architectural stack of the implementation can be seen in

Figure 4.1. This system was designed and implemented to be generic so that
it could run any Unix based platform that has the Docker engine installed.

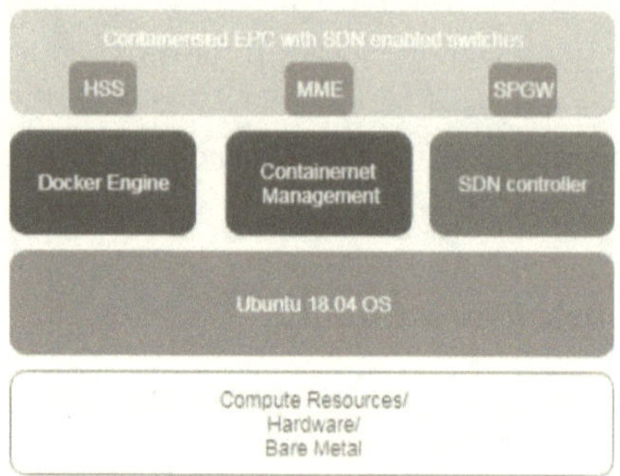


Figure 4.1: Architectural stack used to implement the network environment

## 4.2 SDN Controller

There are many different implementations of network controllers. A full
technical breakdown of the network controller is presented in Appendix A.3.
A comparison of three main network controllers considered can be found in
Table A.1. Based on the information obtained on the different choices of network controllers, it was decided that RYU would be the network controller
utilised in this research because of its popularity in the research space and
its proven track record for quickly creating Proof of Concepts (PoC).

The Flow Request Processor and the Flow Rule Installer in Figure 3.2
are elements built into the functionality of the RYU controller. These functionalities are leveraged via the RYU Python API.

## 4.3 Network Application

This section describes the functional elements utilised by the NIPS network
application in greater detail. All the logical units seen in the Applications

layer of Figure 3.2 are presented in this section. The functions were implemented in a Python script that was included as a new module for the RYU controller. The full sequence of events that are handled by this application can be found in Figure 4.2 and all steps referred to in the remainder of this section refers to the the steps shown in this diagram.

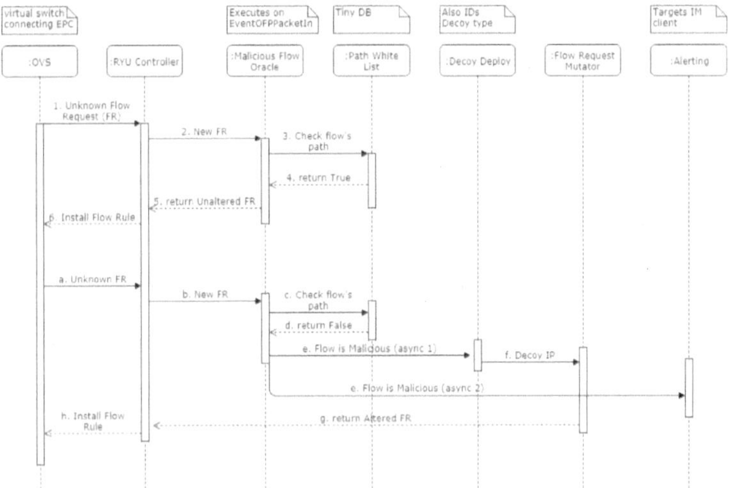


Figure 4.2: Sequence diagram for legitimate flows (1-6) and malicious flows (a-h)

### 4.3.1 Path White list

In the initial setup of the EPC network environment, all the OVS switches will have no flow rules installed in their flow tables. In order for the EPC to function correctly, the elements need to be able to communicate with one another over network paths that are presented in the EPC's technical definition (see Figure 2.1) [22]. Switches in an SDN environment are simplified and limited to only having a flow table of known flows, in order to get the flow rules installed in the switches, the switch needs to reach out to the controller with the unknown flow request (Steps 1. and a.), the controller would then process the request and reply with the appropriate flow rule (Steps 6. and h.).

The NIPS application will be affecting every flow request that is made to the RYU controller via the OVS switches. Therefore it is essential for the the NIPS application to know which flow requests should not get altered by it or trigger alerts. In order to do this, a white list of the network paths that are constantly being utilised by a functioning EPC needs to be created.

This white list of paths will need to be created and configured before the launching of the NIPS application onto the system. The white list will ensure that the EPC's functionalities will not be affected when the NIPS application is running. The white list was created based which EPC HVAs need to communicate with one another

The white list was implemented as a TinyDB database which is a Python database library that creates a JSON based file containing the input information and allows for very fast and simple queries to be performed [54]. For each network path there are two hosts addresses given as the path definition. The path is reversible so therefore a path between HostA and HostB is the same as the path between HostB and HostA.

### 4.3.2 Malicious Flow Oracle

Whenever an OVS switch in the system reaches out to the controller for a flow rule, the controller needs to pass that flow request up to the Applications layer so that the flow can be classified. In order to achieve that, a Python function is written that is called every time an OpenFlow message with event type EventOFPPacketIn is received by the RYU controller (Steps 2. and b.). This function is what will be triggered every time a switch reaches out to the controller with a flow request.

The classifying function is required to extract the network path from the incoming flow request and then compare that path to the white list (Steps

3. and c.). This is done by getting the source and destination values from
the flow request object. The output from the function needs to be a deter-
mination as to whether the flow is malicious or not. In order to determine
whether the flow is malicious, the white list database is queried as to whether
it contains the path extracted from the flow request. If the query returns a
false boolean value, then the flow can be deemed to be malicious (Step d.).
If the query returns a boolean value of true then the flow is not malicious
(Step 4.). In the case that the flow is not malicious then the system simply
allows the RYU controller to process the flow request as is (Steps 5. and 6.).

In the case of the flow being malicious, the Python application kicks off
two separate functionalities asynchronously (Both steps e.). They are detailed in Sections 4.3.3 and 4.3.4 below. The breakdown of the asynchronous
functionality of the network application is found in Section 4.3.5. In the case
of the case of malicious lateral movement from the compromised node to an
HVA across a white listed path then the NIPS functionality would not get
triggered.

## 4.3.3 Decoy process

First asynchronous function is to deploy the decoy node and reroute the
flow towards the decoy. This process has three separate logical functions as
detailed below

**Decoy Type Identifier**

The exact type of the EPC entity that is being targeted needs to be determined so that the correct type of decoy is deployed. The destination param-
eter from the flow request will give the address of the targeted node. From
that address the configuration of the network setup (described in Section 4.4)
is queried to get the type of the node associated with that address.

**Decoy Deployer**

Once the type of decoy required is known, the Python Docker library is used to deploy the decoy [55]. This involves launching another, separate, container from the same docker image as the target. The network address assigned to this container is variablized and stored for usage in the next logical function (Step f.).

**Flow Request Mutator**

The flow request object is then dynamically altered by changing the initial destination address to the address of the freshly deployed decoy (Step g.). Once the flow request has been mutated, the altered flow request is processed by the RYU controller (Step h.), thus installing a flow rule on the network switch that will cause all future data attempting to flow along that same path to be redirected to the decoy.

### 4.3.4 Alerting process

The second asynchronous process that gets triggered when a flow request is determined to be malicious is the sending of alerts to the corresponding MNO operatives. Many channels exist to send the alerts; e.g., email or triggering a digital operations management service specialising in incident response such as PagerDuty. For simplicity sake alerts are sent as Instant Messages (IMs). The chosen IM was Slack. Once the alert gets triggered the Python Slack library is used to connect to the preconfigured slack server and send the alert message to the relevant alerting channel [56].

### 4.3.5 Asynchronous Breakdown

Asynchronous programming involves a single processing thread that places events into a queue and processes them sequentially based on specific event handlers. Asynchronous processing also ensures that whenever one of the two processes experiences a long running step due to a required waiting period for another system/function to reply, then that stream can be placed into a deferred state that allows the other process stream to carry on being processed. Once the deferred stream returns back an expected result, it immediately jumps back to the front of the event queue to be next in line to be completed. This ensures that both functions get completed as quickly as possible, which is essential because both functions covered by Sections 4.3.3 and 4.3.4 are required to be completed quickly. The processing times experienced by the two asynchronous processes can be seen in Figure 4.3.

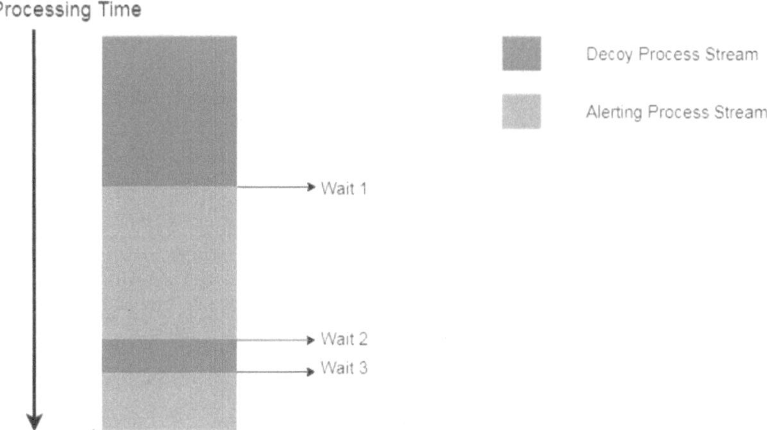


Figure 4.3: Processor time spent on the two asynchronous process streams

The waits in Figure 4.3 can be seen as moments in time when the process stream changes. Wait 1 was determined to be caused by the container deployment which can take up to a couple of seconds. While the docker container is getting deployed the asynchronous system is able to then begin processing the alerting process. The Decoy Process stream is set to being deferred at this point.

Wait 2 was experienced by connecting to the IM server used for alerting. At this point the deferred Decoy Process stream has returned successful deployment and this stream completes.

The connection to the IM server requires a full TCP connection be setup over networks with slow Round Trip Times (RTT). This slow RTT is due to the IM server's being located in the USA while the client is in South Africa. The Alert stream gets deferred while waiting for the server connection. When the IM server is co-located with the EPC deployment then the RTT becomes insignificant.

Wait 3 causes a process stream switch because the Decoy Process stream has completed. At this point the Alerting Process stream has successfully connected to the IM server and can therefore complete all the remaining steps in this process stream.

## 4.4  Network Setup

A simple network topology was used for testing setup via Containernet, five nodes are connected via one switch. Larger topologies with more switches would not make any difference to the overall functionality of the PoC as each OVS switch added would behave in the same way. The EPC nodes added to the network are the basic nodes necessary for an EPC to function correctly. They are the HSS, the MME, the SPGW and the bastion host that would be considered the compromised node in the network. A virtual enodeB is also included that will emulate typical traffic that is experienced by the EPC [57]. The topology can be seen in Figure 4.4.

Docker allows for containers to communicate directly to one another through a bridge/network that is setup internally in the Docker Engine. It was decided to not use this way to connect the EPC containers and to rather connect them via an OVS switch so that the EPC could be SDN enabled and the switches could communicate with the SDN controller, which was essential

for the NIPS application. This connection can be seen in Figure 4.4 as the
OpenFlow link.

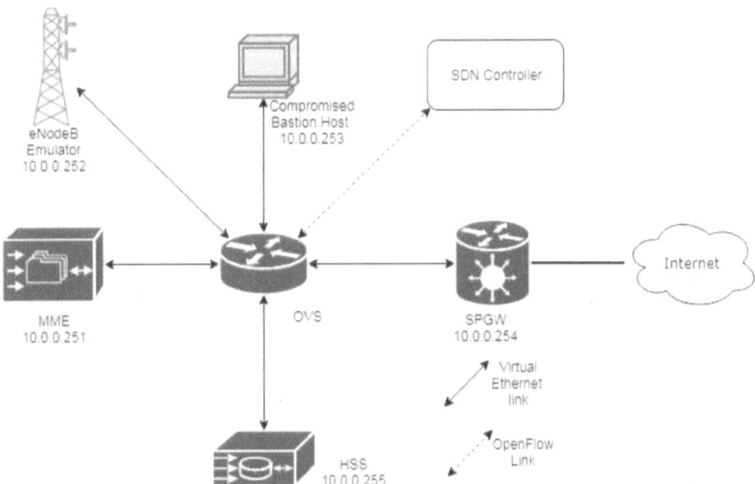


Figure 4.4: Network topology set up in Containernet

A Python script was used to set up the network correctly. The script
ensured that the exact same network layout was created every time the network was setup. This ensured that each host would get the same IP address
whenever the network was deployed as can be seen in Figure 4.4. The script
contained hard coded variables relating the EPC host entities and their corresponding network addresses that they would be deployed with.

The compromised bastion host was created as a basic Ubuntu:18.04 docker
container that had SSH and nmap capabilities. The compromised host only
needed to make simple network calls in order to test the NIPS PoC. The
nmap was included for the use case of network wide scanning to simulate a
network scan that an attacker may use to perform network reconnaissance
[58] as discussed in Section 4.5.3.

## 4.5 Evaluation Techniques

In order to evaluate the effectiveness of the NIPS PoC that was implemented, first the EPC's functionality was validated, then two different attacker patterns were attempted. The first direct contact consists of a simple network request originating from the compromised node towards a node along a non critical path. The second would be for the compromised node to perform a full network scan. The full technical details for how the NIPS application was setup in order to evaluate it's effectiveness is presented in Appendix E.

### 4.5.1 EPC validation

The network connections across critical network paths were first checked in order to test the EPC's functionality. If an EPC node could send an ICMP ping to every other EPC node that it needs to communicate with without triggering the NIPS functionality then the network connections between nodes were deemed traversable. This test needs to be performed across every single network path included in the white list. Basic tests of the interfaces between the EPC elements need to be validated as well, for example the S6a interface between MME and the HSS [23].

The enodeB emulator was included in the network topology in order to emulate the typical traffic that an EPC receives from a RAN. This emulator can simulate multiple Internet based requests that would be managed by the virtual EPC setup in the test network. If this emulator is able to run correctly without triggering the NIPS functionality on the PoC network then the EPC can be considered to be functioning correctly.

### 4.5.2 Direct Network attack

This use case covers the scenario for the attacker knowing the exact network address of their target node in the EPC; they may have found this address inside logs or in a configuration file found on the compromised node. The example covered for this use case would be for the compromised node to directly access the HSS node of the EPC. The NIPS application would be setup in such a way as not to include that direct path in its white list.

The simplest test for this type of attack would be for a simple ICMP ping to be sent to the IP address assigned to the HSS node from the compromised node. This simple test will determine whether the NIPS application would correctly get triggered due to the non critical network path getting requested from the OVS device.

The other direct network attack simulation to be performed would be for the compromised node to attempt to establish an SSH session with the HSS. This test was expected to trigger the same functionality from the NIPS PoC but more feedback would be given to the compromised node while interacting with the attempted SSH connection. This was done in order to determine how convincing the decoy can be.

### 4.5.3  Network scan

In the case of a node getting compromised and the attacker not knowing the layout of the network, the attacker would need to perform reconnaissance such as a full network scan. In order to do this, the compromised node was preconfigured with the nmap utility and a full scan of the entire network range was performed. This full network scan loops over the list of addresses within the same ip address range as the compromised host. For each address within that range, multiple requests are made of that address. If there is no host responding from the current IP address then the host is either assumed powered off or non reachable. The scan of each address returns all open ports on any host that is reachable.

The scanning test will strain the NIPS application as it is expected to involve deploying multiple decoys. Full network scans are known to take a significant amount of time (minutes) as many address and ports are being probed. This will allow for some leeway in terms of how much extra delay is incurred when the NIPS application reacts to the network scan by deploying multiple decoys. With the white list set up in order to emulate the layout presented in Figure 1.2 the only allowed path from the compromised node would be to the MME. Therefore the scan should cause the NIPS to deploy and reroute to a decoy of every other type of EPC node.

There are only a limited amount of entities that are included in the EPC specification. Therefore the chances of a rogue node causing the NIPS to experience a DoS are low as the system would only ever need to deploy as one decoy per EPC entity. If the NIPS were applied to larger networks, checks could be put in place to set an upper limit of decoys to deploy before rather terminating connections from the rogue node all together.

## 4.6   Chapter Discussions

This chapter presented the implementation of the NIPS PoC including all the elements at each of the three SDN layers. The network topology and environment needed in order to achieve the requirements for a successful PoC were also presented. Finally the evaluation techniques were proposed that would validate the effectiveness of the PoC while also ensuring that the PoC implementation does not hinder the EPC's functionality.

The following chapter will detail the results obtained when evaluating the NIPS application PoC. The user journeys that will be experienced by the attacker when triggering the NIPS as well as for the MNO operatives when being alerted to the attackers' actions will also be included.

# Chapter 5

# Results and Discussion

The previous chapter detailed the implementation of the NIPS application and the network environment required to validate the NIPS application. The techniques that would be used to validate the effectiveness of the NIPS application were also covered previously. This chapter provides the outcome of all the evaluations as well as discussing how these outcomes give an indication of the effectiveness of the NIPS application.

## 5.1 EPC Validation

To validate that the EPC was still functioning while interacting with the NIPS application, first a basic ICMP ping was sent along every network path that was included in the white list. This ensured that all the network paths that were critical to the EPC's functionality were still traversable without triggering any of the NIPS application's functionalities.

The Python script that was used to setup the Containernet topology was also utilised to test all the critical pathways in the EPC. This involved pings being sent from one host to another in both directions automatically every time the network environment was deployed. Simple print statements were added into the NIPS application that would give feedback whenever the Malicious Flow Oracle function realised that the flow request was not malicious. Figure 5.1 shows the NIPS application output (Left terminal) with the print statements. Also shown in Figure 5.1 is the critical path checks being performed on the network environment (Right terminal) with the paths being checked in the lines following "*** Testing connectivity". Note that "flow is not malicious" was printed six times (Left) and six pathways were tested (Right)

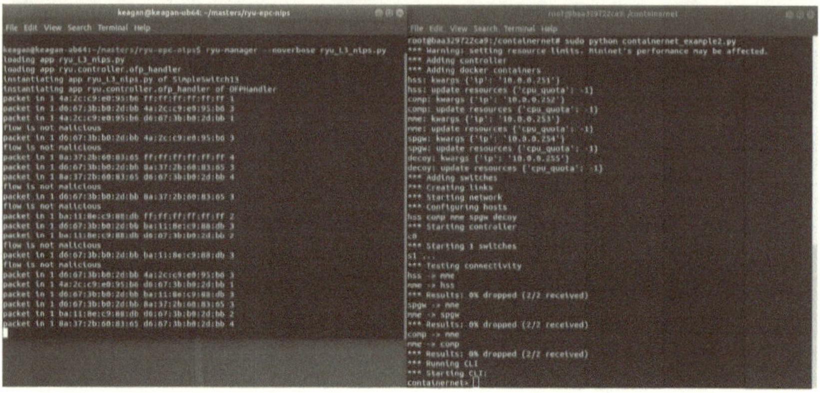

Figure 5.1: Critical paths being checked on the network environment deployment

Next the basic EPC functionalities needed to be tested, this was done by viewing the running interactions between the EPC VNFs across the predefined bearers. The first example of these can be seen in Figures 5.2, which shows the SPGW's initial setup to be able to handle the GPRS tunneling protocol as well as the S11 interface being initialised for communication with the MME. Figure 5.3 then shows the S6a bearer being successfully traversed allowing for the MME (Purple lines) and HSS (Green lines) entities to interact correctly.

Figure 5.2: Combination of the SGW and PGW deploying as a singular SPGW entity

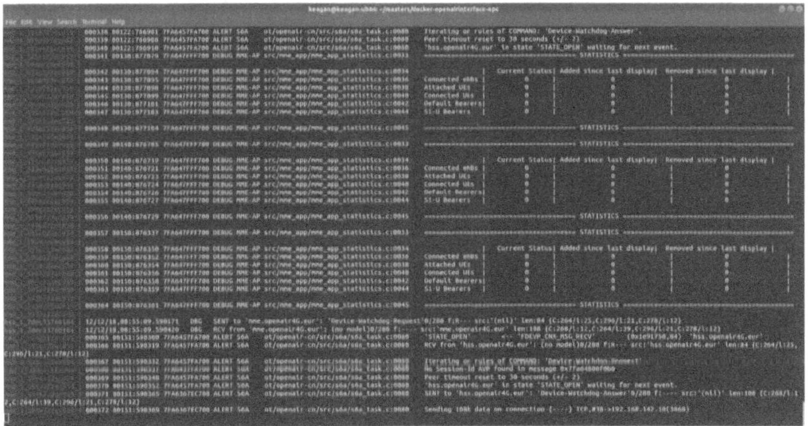

Figure 5.3: MME and HSS interactions across the S6a bearer

The EPC's overall functionality was also tested by connecting an enodeB emulator that would simulate traffic through the network (refer to Figure 4.4). This test was done on a standard deployment of the EPC with a simple switch and again on the EPC deployment that was interacting with the NIPS application. There was no difference found in the functionalities of both these types of EPC deployments. The NIPS application was never triggered during the test including the enodeB, concluding that the NIPS application was functioning as expected during normal EPC functionalities.

## 5.2   Direct Attack

For the direct network attack to be verified, a non critical pathway needed to be traversed. The path chosen for this test was the pathway between the compromised node and the HSS node. This path was not included in the white list used by the NIPS application.

Any type of network traffic between these two nodes would be triggering the NIPS application's functionality, therefore a simple ping request was sent from the compromised node to the HSS node. Ping requests have the added benefit of outputting the time taken for the ping to reach its destination and return back to the source. The time taken for the pings to complete their round trip (RTT) was therefore chosen as the metric to measure the success of the NIPS application against a direct attack because attackers would notice large delays incurred in their network requests when attempting lateral movement.

Figure 5.4 shows both the output from the NIPS application (Left Terminal) as well as the user journey experienced by the attacker when attempting to ping the HSS from the compromised node (Right terminal). The left terminal illustrates that once a malicious flow is detected by the NIPS application, the alerting system and the decoy deployment are carried out as well as redirecting the flow towards the decoy. The right terminal shows that the attacker would not receive any errors when attempting to reach the HSS directly, and the ping request is completed successfully.

In this case illustrated in Figure 5.4 only a single ping was sent. This shows that the very first request sent along the non critical path takes on average 2.8 seconds which is made longer due to the overhead added to the controller's processing time by the NIPS application's functionalities. This overhead is only ever experienced on the first traversal of that non critical network path. Subsequent pings returned with an average time of 50ms because the switch already has the correct flow rule installed in its flow table and does not need to reach out to the controller. Initial pings across non-malicious flows were also analysed and were found to have an average time of 1.4 seconds. This overhead is due to the overhead of the switch reaching out to the controller.

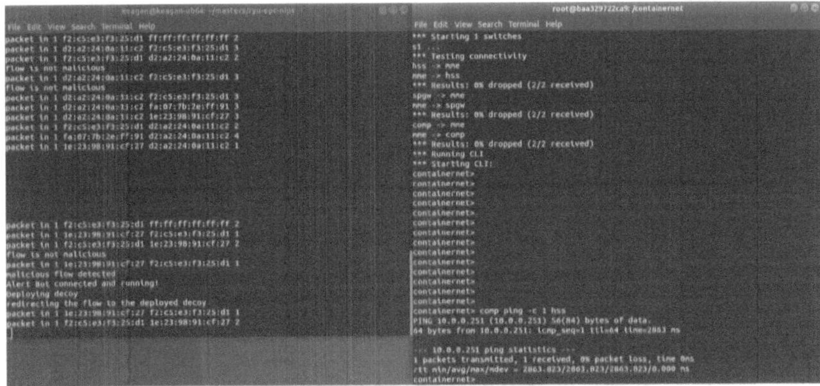

Figure 5.4: Direct network attack being simulated from compromised node to HSS

The IM based alerting can be seen in Figure 5.5. Note that only singular messages were sent whenever malicious flows were detected, therefore preventing the channel getting flooded. This single message is due to the fact that only the initial packet in a malicious flow triggers the NIPS application and all subsequent packets flow freely through the switch to the decoy as discussed above.

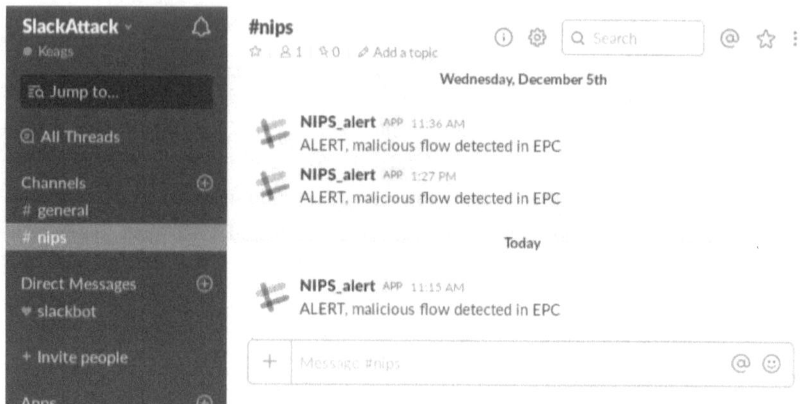



Figure 5.5: Alert messages as viewed in the Slack IM client application

To further evaluate the NIPS application's validity against a direct attack, an SSH session was attempted from the compromised node to the HSS. Figure 5.6 details the output that would be experienced by the attacker when attempting to SSH across a non critical path. SSH server is not running on any of the nodes other than the decoy that gets deployed therefore the only host that could be responding to the SSH connection correctly is the decoy. This shows that the compromised node attempted to SSH onto the HSS (by using the ip address of the HSS), the NIPS was triggered and redirected the flow to the decoy and now all further network interactions by the compromised node would be acting on the decoy node including the remainder of the SSH session. The last line in Figure 5.6 shows the name of the host that was accessed as being the decoy.

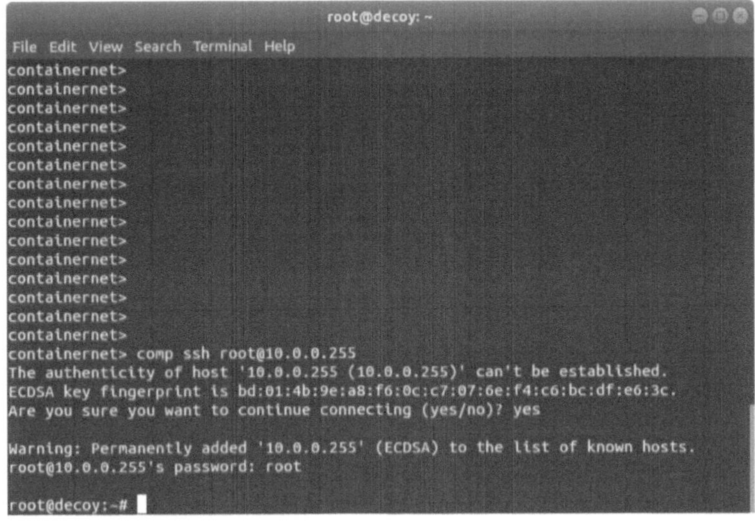

Figure 5.6: Compromised node initiating a SSH session attempting to access the HSS and being rerouted to the decoy

## 5.3　Network Reconnaissance Attack

The last test for the NIPS application's evaluation was for the attacker to perform a network map from the compromised node. Figure 5.7 shows the output experienced by the attacker (Right terminal) as well as the output from the NIPS application (Left terminal) when the Nmap service is used to map the network from the compromised node.

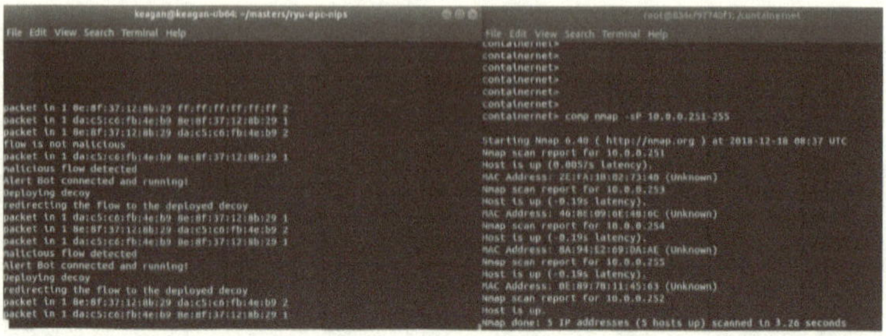

Figure 5.7: Nmap scan being performed

When the compromised node performs the network scan, it triggers two separate decoys to get deployed as can be seen in the left terminal of Figure 5.7. The two decoys that get deployed are the HSS decoy and the SPGW decoy, because there is no critical path between the compromised node and these two entities. No MME decoy gets deployed because the path between the compromised node and the MME was added to the white list of critical paths.

The attacker would see the output generated in the right terminal which appears to be a successful nmap scan detailing the five nodes available in the current EPC network. After the network scan was performed, when the compromised node attempts to contact the HSS or the SPGW directly, those network flows would get redirected to the decoys.

## 5.4   Chapter Discussions

This chapter presented the validation of the effectiveness of the NIPS application first in terms of determining that the EPC still functioned correctly when interacting with the NIPS. Secondly it detailed the effectiveness of the NIPS application against two separate types of attacks that can be performed from a compromised node inside the EPC.

The EPC was validated first by proving that all the paths that are critical to the EPC's functionalities were traversable by simple ICMP ping packets. This was done across all the paths that were added to the NIPS application's white list of critical paths.

Next the specific interactions between the EPC entities were shown to be functioning correctly. This was shown both during initialisation of the EPC as well as during normal operational loads expected by the EPC by means of an enodeB emulator.

The first attack type that the NIPS was tested against was the direct attack where the compromised node was attempting to directly contact the HSS of the EPC. This network path was explicitly excluded from the NIPS application's white list. The RTT for the pings was used as a metric to measure how quickly the NIPS application could react to the detected malicious flow. It was observed that the first ping would take on average 2.8 seconds due to the fact that the NIPS application needed to deploy the decoy first before altering the flow request. This initial delay could cause suspicion to be raised by the attacker. All subsequent pings were seen to take an average of 50ms therefore illustrating that the switch did not need to reach out to the controller again and the compromised node was having its network traffic redirected to the decoy node.

The SSH example showed that the attacker would experience a typical user journey when attempting to SSH onto the HSS from the compromised node whereas in actual fact they are SSH'ing onto the decoy.

The second attack type used to verify the NIPS's effectiveness was the network scan. It was shown that when the compromised node performs the scan, decoys get deployed of the entities which the compromised node should not be able to contact. The attacker will see their network scan complete successfully on the whole EPC network but they would not have been able to scan the HSS or the SPGW and are only interacting with the decoy versions of those entities.

The next chapter will present the conclusion as well as recommendations
for future work.

# Chapter 6

# Conclusion and Recommendations

The previous chapters presented the background, design, implementation and the verification of the NIPS for the EPC. This chapter summarizes the research, presents recommendations for future work and concludes this work.

## 6.1 Summary

The EPC is a fundamental component to MNOs, therefore it is important that the proposed system does not affect the EPC's functionalities. A thorough background was presented that detailed the architecture of a basic EPC and its functionalities. This was done in order to gain a better understanding of the network interactions between the EPC entities. From this understanding came the ability to discern between critical and non critical paths within an EPC setup. A literature review was presented that detailed the usage of the SDN and NFV paradigms in other research relating to the EPC and network security. They were shown to have been used for similar use cases but never for the exact case of preventing an attacker from moving laterally throughout the EPC.

The requirements for the NIPS application were detailed in Chapter 3.

These requirements described how the NIPS application should not interfere with the EPC's functionalities while still being able to detect, contain
and respond to attackers attempting lateral movement within the EPC. The
design of the NIPS application was also presented including a view of the
functional elements that were required as viewed from a SDN architecture
stand point.

Chapter 4 presented how the NIPS application was implemented. The
functions implemented for each layer of the SDN architecture were described
in high levels of technical details. This chapter also detailed the technical
steps required to create a network environment suitable for testing of the
NIPS application. The techniques that would be used to validate the effectiveness of the NIPS application were described including methods to validate
the EPC as well as describing two types of attacks that would be conducted.

Finally, Chapter 5 presented the outcomes of the evaluation techniques.
This chapter showed that the EPC functions as designed while having the
NIPS application interacting with its network. The NIPS application was
also shown to successfully detect both types of attacks while automatically
triggering responses to the detected attack by containing the attack and
alerting MNO operatives.

## 6.2   Recommendations

This **book** presented a NIPS application that made use of SDN and NFV
techniques to protect the EPC from attackers that had compromised a node
within the mobile Core Network. The NIPS's functionalities could be
added to in multiple ways to give more helpful feedback and be more deceptive when dealing with attackers. More extensive evaluation techniques for
the NIPS are also worth exploring.

The first recommendation would be to improve the 2.8 second average
time taken for the first ping in the direct attack. This delay is noticeable

when attempting a direct attack and could tip the attacker off that their actions have triggered an automated alarm system. The delay was found to mostly be cause by the deployment of the decoy. The flow rule could not be mutated and installed onto the switch before the decoy had successfully been deployed, if it was installed before the deployment completed, the pings would be unsuccessful as they would be directed to a host that does not yet have networking services running. Therefore the decoy deployment became a blocking process.

There are two ways that this blocking process could be improved. The first would be to deploy a more light weight decoy. A very basic container that has minimal overhead and only pretends to be a fully functioning EPC entity by listening on the correct ports would get deployed much quicker therefore lowering the delay incurred in the first ping of a direct attack.

The second way to completely remove the blocking process would be to have the decoys constantly being deployed. This option has the down side that most of the time these decoy containers would be utilising computing resources while not performing any function for the MNOs. The benefit of this approach is that as soon as a malicious flow is detected the flow can get redirected to the decoy without any need for the blocking process of deploying the decoy. This method would practically eliminate the 2.8 second delay experienced by the first ping of the direct attack evaluation.

A further recommendation would be for the IM alerting messages to be more informative about which node instigated the malicious flow, therefore pointing the MNO operatives to the compromised node. This information is obtainable from the flow request that is available to the NIPS application. It was noticed that when the network scan was performed, multiple alert messages were sent that could be customised to mention the target of the attacks. This would also give the MNO operatives information about their attacker as they could discern whether the attacker was mapping their network or actively trying to directly contact a HVA of the EPC.

In order to be more deceptive, the host names of the decoys should be changed to be more specific to the type of node they are decoying as. This would prevent the attacker from seeing "root@decoy" such as the last line of Figure 5.6.

The NIPS application could be run in unison with another system that can more closely monitor the traffic along critical network paths. This could involve some form of DPI on the critical paths that would be able to verify that only legitimate EPC generated traffic is traversing the critical paths. This would make lateral movement of any kind highly difficult for attackers of the EPC.

When the NIPS is applied to an EPC the risk of DoS is very low. If the NIPS were to be applied to other larger networks, then an upper limit needs to be created for decoys per malicious node in order to prevent a DoS of the NIPS.

A Network Address Translation rule could be applied to return packets from the decoy node such that the return packets seen by the compromised node would be seen as the targeted HVA's address.

The final recommendation would be for the NIPS application to be applied to a fully fledged EPC that has all the entities integrated that an MNO would have, this would include Authentication, Authorization, and Accounting (AAA), Policy and Charging Rules Function (PCRF), Policy and Charging Enforcement Function (PCEF), and all other EPC entities used to support legacy systems. As more of these entities are added to the EPC, the amount of non critical paths grow at an exponential rate. As the percentage of non critical to critical network paths grows larger, so too does the probability of the attacker making a false step and triggering the NIPS. A network map attack performed on a fully fledged EPC would be a great stress test for the NIPS application as a large amount of decoys would have to be deployed as well as having to reroute many flows.

## 6.3  Conclusion

In this book, a NIPS for the EPC that leverages off the SDN and NFV paradigms is presented. It was shown that research had been focussed on defending the perimeter of the EPC from attackers and that no research had been performed on defenses that would detect, contain and respond to attackers that had bypassed the perimeter defenses and managed to compromise a node within the EPC.

This research shows that by setting up a system that only allows for critical network paths between the entities of the EPC to be traversed, it is possible to create a proactive defence against would be attackers of the EPC, as opposed to a reactive one. The SDN paradigm allows for network applications to have a global network view, as well as a programmatic interface to allow direct control of the network's forwarding devices. This allows for the NIPS application to monitor the state of the network controller for malicious flows. Once malicious flows are detected, automated alerting can be sent out while asynchronously containing the compromised node by rerouting its malicious flows to a decoy that was deployed using NFV techniques. As far as the author is aware, this is the first implementation of an SDN and NFV based NIPS for the EPC that prevents attackers from moving laterally between entities.

The NIPS was shown to not hinder the functionalities of the EPC that it was protecting while still being able to effectively prevent both direct attacks and network reconnaissance attacks.

Therefore, this book has shown that the NIPS application is a valid means of defending the EPC from attackers that compromised a node within the EPC, while still allowing the EPC to function correctly.

# REFERENCES

[1] L. Chang, D. R. B. S. Hill, and K. Wiggers. "Mobile." URL http://www.digitaltrends.com/mobile/mobile-phone-world-population-2014/.

[2] C. Arthur. "Mobile internet devices 'will outnumber humans this year'.", Feb 2013. URL https://www.theguardian.com/technology/2013/feb/07/mobile-internet-outnumber-people.

[3] J. Jermyn, R. P. Jover, M. Istomin, and I. Murynets. "Firecycle: A scalable test bed for large-scale LTE security research." In *2014 IEEE International Conference on Communications (ICC)*, pp. 907–913. June 2014.

[4] S. Mavoungou, G. Kaddoum, M. Taha, and G. Matar. "Survey on Threats and Attacks on Mobile Networks." *IEEE Access*, vol. 4, pp. 4543–4572, 2016.

[5] J. Pepitone. "Dropbox's password nightmare highlights cloud risks.", June 2011. URL http://money.cnn.com/2011/06/22/technology/dropbox_passwords/index.htm.

[6] W. Hu, L. Zhang, A. Ardeshiricham, J. Blackstone, B. Hou, Y. Tai, and R. Kastner. "Why you should care about don't cares: Exploiting internal don't care conditions for hardware Trojans." In *2017 IEEE/ACM International Conference on Computer-Aided Design (IC-CAD)*, pp. 707–713. Nov 2017.

[7] NIST. "Software Supply Chain Attacks.", 2017. URL `https://csrc.nist.gov/CSRC/media/Projects/Supply-Chain-Risk-Management/documents/ssca/2017-winter/NCSC_Placemat.pdf`.

[8] S. Scott-Hayward, G. O'Callaghan, and S. Sezer. "Sdn Security: A Survey." In *2013 IEEE SDN for Future Networks and Services (SDN4FNS)*, pp. 1–7. Nov 2013.

[9] A. Badea, V. Croitoru, and D. Gheorghica. "Computer network vulnerabilities and monitoring." In *2015 9th International Symposium on Advanced Topics in Electrical Engineering (ATEE)*, pp. 49–54. May 2015.

[10] J. Xu, X. Yuan, A. Yu, J. H. Kim, T. Kim, and J. Zhang. "Developing and evaluating a hands-on lab for teaching local area network vulnerabilities." In *2016 IEEE Frontiers in Education Conference (FIE)*, pp. 1–4. Oct 2016.

[11] T. Xing, D. Huang, L. Xu, C. J. Chung, and P. Khatkar. "SnortFlow: A OpenFlow-Based Intrusion Prevention System in Cloud Environment." In *2013 Second GENI Research and Educational Experiment Workshop*, pp. 89–92. March 2013.

[12] O. I. S. Foundation. "Open Source IDS / IPS / NSM engine.", 2018. URL `https://suricata-ids.org/`.

[13] R. Gopakumar, A. M. Unni, and V. P. Dhipin. "An adaptive algorithm for searching in flow tables of openflow switches." In *2015 39th National Systems Conference (NSC)*, pp. 1–5. Dec 2015.

[14] J. D. D. Marschke and P. Moyer. *Software Defined Networking (SDN): Anatomy of OpenFlow*. Lulu Publishing Advances in Health Economics and Health Services Research, 2015.

[15] C. Bouras, A. Kollia, and A. Papazois. "SDN NFV in 5G: Advancements and challenges." In *2017 20th Conference on Innovations in Clouds, Internet and Networks (ICIN)*, pp. 107–111. March 2017.

[16] H. Solomon. "Networks Face 'Crisis of Trust': Websense, it World Canada.", 2013. URL https://www.itworldcanada.com/article/networks-face-crisis-of-trust-websense/47411.

[17] S. T. Ali, V. Sivaraman, A. Radford, and S. Jha. "A Survey of Securing Networks Using Software Defined Networking." *IEEE Transactions on Reliability*, vol. 64, no. 3, pp. 1086–1097, Sept 2015.

[18] I. Ahmad, T. Kumar, M. Liyanage, J. Okwuibe, M. Ylianttila, and A. Gurtov. "5G security: Analysis of threats and solutions." In *2017 IEEE Conference on Standards for Communications and Networking (CSCN)*, pp. 193–199. Sept 2017.

[19] I. Ahmad, T. Kumar, M. Liyanage, J. Okwuibe, M. Ylianttila, and A. Gurtov. "Overview of 5G Security Challenges and Solutions." *IEEE Communications Standards Magazine*, vol. 2, no. 1, pp. 36–43, MARCH 2018.

[20] S. GALLAGHER. "NSA let Snowden crawl all over its intranet unchecked.", 2014. URL https://arstechnica.com/information-technology/2014/02/nsa-let-snowden-crawl-all-over-its-intranet-unchecked/.

[21] H. M. J. Almohri, L. T. Watson, and D. Evans. "Misery Digraphs: Delaying Intrusion Attacks in Obscure Clouds." *IEEE Transactions on Information Forensics and Security*, vol. 13, no. 6, pp. 1361–1375, June 2018.

[22] J. Kempf, B. Johansson, S. Pettersson, H. Luning, and T. Nilsson. "Moving the mobile Evolved Packet Core to the cloud." In *Wireless and Mobile Computing, Networking and Communications (WiMob), 2012 IEEE 8th International Conference on*, pp. 784–791. Oct 2012.

[23] E. B. Hamza and S. Kimura. "A Scalable SDN-EPC Architecture Based on OpenFlow-Enabled Switches to Support Inter-domain Handover." In *2016 10th International Conference on Innovative Mobile*

*and Internet Services in Ubiquitous Computing (IMIS)*, pp. 272–277. July 2016.

[24] T. Q. Thanh, D. Vingarzan, Y. Rebahi, and T. Magedanz. "A Diameter based testing system in Next Generation Mobile Network." In *2010 14th International Telecommunications Network Strategy and Planning Symposium (NETWORKS)*, pp. 1–5. Sep. 2010.

[25] J. Nikolai and Y. Wang. "A System for Detecting Malicious Insider Data Theft in IaaS Cloud Environments." In *2016 IEEE Global Communications Conference (GLOBECOM)*, pp. 1–6. Dec 2016.

[26] M. B. Salem, S. Hershkop, and S. J. Stolfo. *A Survey of Insider Attack Detection Research*, pp. 69–90. Boston, MA: Springer US, 2008. URL `https://doi.org/10.1007/978-0-387-77322-3{_}5`.

[27] M. Paolini. "Wireless Security in LTE Networks.", 2012. URL `http://www.gsma.com/membership/wp-content/uploads/2012/11/SenzaFili_WirelessSecurity_121029_FINAL.pdf`.

[28] M. Liyanage, A. B. Abro, M. Ylianttila, and A. Gurtov. "Opportunities and Challenges of Software-Defined Mobile Networks in Network Security." *IEEE Security Privacy*, vol. 14, no. 4, pp. 34–44, July 2016.

[29] S. Park, S. Kim, J. Oh, M. Noh, and C. Im. "Threats and Countermeasures on a 4G Mobile Network." In *2014 Eighth International Conference on Innovative Mobile and Internet Services in Ubiquitous Computing*, pp. 538–541. July 2014.

[30] T. Q. Thanh, Y. Rebahi, and T. Magedanz. "A DIAMETER based security framework for mobile networks." In *2014 International Conference on Telecommunications and Multimedia (TEMU)*, pp. 7–12. July 2014.

[31] E. FP7-ICT. "NEMESYS Project - Enhanced Network Security for Seamless Service Provisioning in the Smart Mobile Ecosystem.", 2014. URL `http://www.nemesys-project.eu/nemesys`.

[32] BMBF. "ASMONIA Project - Attack analysis and Security concepts for MObile Network infrastructures, supported by collaborative Information exchAnge.", 2013. URL `http://asmonia.de`.

[33] K. Bakshi. "Considerations for Software Defined Networking (SDN): Approaches and use cases." In *2013 IEEE Aerospace Conference*, pp. 1–9. March 2013.

[34] K. K. Nguyen and M. Cheriet. "Enabling infrastructure as a service (IaaS) on IP networks: from distributed to virtualized control plane." *IEEE Communications Magazine*, vol. 51, no. 1, pp. 136–144, January 2013.

[35] R. Klöti, V. Kotronis, and P. Smith. "OpenFlow: A security analysis." In *2013 21st IEEE International Conference on Network Protocols (ICNP)*, pp. 1–6. Oct 2013.

[36] N. da Fonseca and R. Boutaba. *Openflow and SDN for Clouds*, p. 432. Wiley-IEEE Press, 2015. URL `http://ieeexplore.ieee.org/xpl/articleDetails.jsp?arnumber=7090285`.

[37] S. Lal, T. Taleb, and A. Dutta. "NFV: Security Threats and Best Practices." *IEEE Communications Magazine*, vol. PP, no. 99, pp. 2–8, 2017.

[38] M. Liyanage, I. Ahmed, J. Okwuibe, M. Ylianttila, H. Kabir, J. L. Santos, R. Kantola, O. L. Perez, M. U. Itzazelaia, and E. M. D. Oca. "Enhancing Security of Software Defined Mobile Networks." *IEEE Access*, vol. 5, pp. 9422–9438, 2017.

[39] Z. L. H. Han, L. Yan and J. Zhang. ""Network security defense system based on software-defined network and working method of network security defense system." In *Patent CN104539625*. Apr. 22, 2015.

[40] M. Monshizadeh, V. Khatri, and R. Kantola. "Detection as a service: An SDN application." In *2017 19th International Conference on Advanced Communication Technology (ICACT)*, pp. 285–290. Feb 2017.

[41] Y. D. Lin, P. C. Lin, C. H. Yeh, Y. C. Wang, and Y. C. Lai. "An extended SDN architecture for network function virtualization with a case study on intrusion prevention." *IEEE Network*, vol. 29, no. 3, pp. 48–53, May 2015.

[42] L. R. Battula. "Network Security Function Virtualization(NSFV) towards Cloud computing with NFV Over Openflow infrastructure: Challenges and novel approaches." In *2014 International Conference on Advances in Computing, Communications and Informatics (ICACCI)*, pp. 1622–1628. Sept 2014.

[43] H. Jang, J. Jeong, H. Kim, and J. S. Park. "A Survey on Interfaces to Network Security Functions in Network Virtualization." In *2015 IEEE 29th International Conference on Advanced Information Networking and Applications Workshops*, pp. 160–163. March 2015.

[44] M. Monshizadeh, V. Khatri, and A. Gurtov. "NFV security considerations for cloud-based mobile virtual network operators." In *2016 24th International Conference on Software, Telecommunications and Computer Networks (SoftCOM)*, pp. 1–5. Sept 2016.

[45] M. Liyanage, I. Ahmed, M. Ylianttila, J. L. Santos, R. Kantola, O. L. Perez, M. U. Itzazelaia, E. M. d. Oca, A. Valtierra, and C. Jimenez. "Security for Future Software Defined Mobile Networks." In *2015 9th International Conference on Next Generation Mobile Applications, Services and Technologies*, pp. 256–264. Sept 2015.

[46] P. Kim. *The Hacker Playbook*. CreateSpace Independent Publishing Platform, 2014.

[47] V. Sucasas, G. Mantas, and J. Rodriguez. "Security Challenges for Cloud Radio Access Networks.", 09 2016.

[48] T. Q. Thanh, Y. Rebahi, and T. Magedanz. "A DIAMETER based security framework for mobile networks." In *2014 International Conference on Telecommunications and Multimedia (TEMU)*, pp. 7–12. July 2014.

[49] L. Foundation. "Production Quality, Multilayer Open Virtual Switch.", 2018. URL `http://openvswitch.org/`.

[50] "OpenEPC Website.", 2018. URL `https://www.openepc.com`.

[51] J. Fontenla-González, C. Pérez-Garrido, F. Gil-Castiñeira, F. J. González-Castaño, and C. Giraldo-Rodriguez. "Lightweight container-based OpenEPC deployment and its evaluation." In *2016 IEEE NetSoft Conference and Workshops (NetSoft)*, pp. 435–440. June 2016.

[52] Y. C. Tay, K. Gaurav, and P. Karkun. "A Performance Comparison of Containers and Virtual Machines in Workload Migration Context." In *2017 IEEE 37th International Conference on Distributed Computing Systems Workshops (ICDCSW)*, pp. 61–66. June 2017.

[53] M. Peuster, J. Kampmeyer, and H. Karl. "Containernet 2.0: A Rapid Prototyping Platform for Hybrid Service Function Chains." In *2018 4th IEEE Conference on Network Softwarization and Workshops (NetSoft)*, pp. 335–337. June 2018.

[54] M. Siemens. "Welcome to TinyDB!", 2018. URL `https://tinydb.readthedocs.io/en/latest/`.

[55] D. Inc. "Docker SDK for Python.", 2018. URL `https://docker-py.readthedocs.io/en/stable/`.

[56] I. Slack Technologies. "Slack Developer Kit for Python.", 2018. URL `https://slackapi.github.io/python-slackclient/`.

[57] A. Gopalasingham, D. G. Herculea, C. S. Chen, and L. Roullet. "Virtualization of radio access network by Virtual Machine and Docker: Practice and performance analysis." In *2017 IFIP/IEEE Symposium on Integrated Network and Service Management (IM)*, pp. 680–685. May 2017.

[58] N. Organisation. "Nmap: Prevent security disasters before they happen.", 2018. URL `https://nmap.org/`.

[59] S. Bu, F. R. Yu, X. P. Liu, and H. Tang. "Structural Results for Combined Continuous User Authentication and Intrusion Detection in High Security Mobile Ad-Hoc Networks." *IEEE Transactions on Wireless Communications*, vol. 10, no. 9, pp. 3064–3073, September 2011.

[60] Q. Yan, F. R. Yu, Q. Gong, and J. Li. "Software-Defined Networking (SDN) and Distributed Denial of Service (DDoS) Attacks in Cloud Computing Environments: A Survey, Some Research Issues, and Challenges." *IEEE Communications Surveys Tutorials*, vol. 18, no. 1, pp. 602–622, Firstquarter 2016.

[61] A. G. Kravets and M. Al-Ashval. "Mobile corporate networks security control." In *2016 International Siberian Conference on Control and Communications (SIBCON)*, pp. 1–6. May 2016.

[62] Y. Wan, J. Cao, G. Chen, and W. Huang. "Distributed Observer-Based Cyber-Security Control of Complex Dynamical Networks." *IEEE Transactions on Circuits and Systems I: Regular Papers*, vol. PP, no. 99, pp. 1–10;, 2017.

[63] X. Costa-Perez, J. Swetina, T. Guo, R. Mahindra, and S. Rangarajan. "Radio access network virtualization for future mobile carrier networks." *Communications Magazine, IEEE*, vol. 51, no. 7, pp. 27–35, July 2013.

[64] A. Khan, W. Kellerer, K. Kozu, and M. Yabusaki. "Network sharing in the next mobile network: TCO reduction, management flexibility, and operational independence." *Communications Magazine, IEEE*, vol. 49, no. 10, pp. 134–142, Oct 2011.

[65] L. Li, Z. Mao, and J. Rexford. "Toward Software-Defined Cellular Networks." In *Software Defined Networking (EWSDN), 2012 European Workshop on*, pp. 7–12. Oct 2012.

[66] P. Minoves, O. Frendved, B. Peng, A. Mackarel, and D. Wilson. "Virtual CPE: Enhancing CPE's deployment and operations through virtualization." In *Cloud Computing Technology and Science (CloudCom), 2012 IEEE 4th International Conference on*, pp. 687–692. Dec 2012.

[67] K. Pentikousis, Y. Wang, and W. Hu. "Mobileflow: Toward software-defined mobile networks." *Communications Magazine, IEEE*, vol. 51, no. 7, pp. 44–53, July 2013.

[68] E. Salvadori, R. Doriguzzi Corin, A. Broglio, and M. Gerola. "Generalizing Virtual Network Topologies in OpenFlow-Based Networks." In *Global Telecommunications Conference (GLOBECOM 2011), 2011 IEEE*, pp. 1–6. Dec 2011.

[69] H. Shimonishi and S. Ishii. "Virtualized network infrastructure using OpenFlow." In *Network Operations and Management Symposium Workshops (NOMS Wksps), 2010 IEEE/IFIP*, pp. 74–79. April 2010.

[70] Tellabs. "Tellabs end of profit study executive summary."

[71] H. Woesner and D. Fritzsche. "SDN and OpenFlow for converged access/aggregation networks." In *Optical Fiber Communication Conference and Exposition and the National Fiber Optic Engineers Conference (OFC/NFOEC), 2013*, pp. 1–3. March 2013.

[72] T. Dargahi, A. Caponi, M. Ambrosin, G. Bianchi, and M. Conti. "A Survey on the Security of Stateful SDN Data Planes." *IEEE Communications Surveys Tutorials*, vol. PP, no. 99, pp. 1–1, 2017.

[73] M. Liyanage, I. Ahmad, M. Ylianttila, A. Gurtov, A. B. Abro, and E. M. de Oca. "Leveraging LTE security with SDN and NFV." In *2015 IEEE 10th International Conference on Industrial and Information Systems (ICIIS)*, pp. 220–225. Dec 2015.

[74] J. Anderson, H. Hu, U. Agarwal, C. Lowery, H. Li, and A. Apon. "Performance considerations of network functions virtualization using con-

tainers." In *2016 International Conference on Computing, Networking and Communications (ICNC)*, pp. 1–7. Feb 2016.

[75] J. Struye, B. Spinnewyn, K. Spaey, K. Bonjean, and S. Latre. "Assessing the value of containers for NFVs: A detailed network performance study." In *2017 13th International Conference on Network and Service Management (CNSM)*, pp. 1–7. Nov 2017.

[76] O. E. Ekene, R. Ruhl, and P. Zavarsky. "Enhanced User Security and Privacy Protection in 4G LTE Network." In *2016 IEEE 40th Annual Computer Software and Applications Conference (COMPSAC)*, vol. 2, pp. 443–448. June 2016.

[77] R. P. Jover. "Security attacks against the availability of LTE mobility networks: Overview and research directions." In *2013 16th International Symposium on Wireless Personal Multimedia Communications (WPMC)*, pp. 1–9. June 2013.

[78] T. Wu and G. Gong. "The Weakness of Integrity Protection for LTE." In *Proceedings of the Sixth ACM Conference on Security and Privacy in Wireless and Mobile Networks*, WiSec '13, pp. 79–88. New York, NY, USA: ACM, 2013. URL http://doi.acm.org/10.1145/2462096.2462110.

[79] D. Kreutz, F. M. V. Ramos, P. E. Veríssimo, C. E. Rothenberg, S. Azodolmolky, and S. Uhlig. "Software-Defined Networking: A Comprehensive Survey." *Proceedings of the IEEE*, vol. 103, no. 1, pp. 14–76, Jan 2015.

[80] M. Monshizadeh, Z. Yan, L. Hippeläinen, and V. Khatri. "Cloudification and security implications of TaaS." In *2015 World Symposium on Computer Networks and Information Security (WSCNIS)*, pp. 1–8. Sept 2015.

[81] N. Katanekwa and N. Ventura. "Mobile content distribution and selective traffic offload in the 3GPP evolved packet system (EPS)." In *The*

*International Conference on Information Networking 2013 (ICOIN)*, pp. 119–124. Jan 2013.

[82] S. Sezer, S. Scott-Hayward, P. Chouhan, B. Fraser, D. Lake, J. Finnegan, N. Viljoen, M. Miller, and N. Rao. "Are we ready for SDN? Implementation challenges for software-defined networks." *Communications Magazine, IEEE*, vol. 51, no. 7, pp. 36–43, July 2013.

[83] pp. 1–5, Sept 2007.

[84] I. Ahmad, S. Namal, M. Ylianttila, and A. Gurtov. "Security in Software Defined Networks: A Survey." *IEEE Communications Surveys Tutorials*, vol. 17, no. 4, pp. 2317–2346, Fourthquarter 2015.

[85] M. Shimamura and K. Kono. "Using Attack Information to Reduce False Positives in Network IDS." In *11th IEEE Symposium on Computers and Communications (ISCC'06)*, pp. 386–393. June 2006.

[86] E. Hooper. "An intelligent detection and response strategy to false positives and network attacks: operation of network quarantine channels and feedback methods to IDS." In *Second International Workshop on Security, Privacy and Trust in Pervasive and Ubiquitous Computing (SecPerU'06)*, pp. 6 pp.–21. June 2006.

[87] J. H. Jafarian, E. Al-Shaer, and Q. Duan. "Openflow Random Host Mutation: Transparent Moving Target Defense Using Software Defined Networking." In *Proceedings of the First Workshop on Hot Topics in Software Defined Networks*, HotSDN '12, pp. 127–132. New York, NY, USA: ACM, 2012. URL `http://doi.acm.org/10.1145/2342441.2342467`.

[88] J. P. G. Sterbenz, D. Hutchison, E. K. Çetinkaya, A. Jabbar, J. P. Rohrer, M. Schöller, and P. Smith. "Resilience and Survivability in Communication Networks: Strategies, Principles, and Survey of Disciplines." *Comput. Netw.*, vol. 54, no. 8, pp. 1245–1265, Jun. 2010. URL `http://dx.doi.org/10.1016/j.comnet.2010.03.005`.

[89] L. Zhang, G. Shou, Y. Hu, and Z. Guo. "Deployment of Intrusion Prevention System based on Software Defined Networking." In *2013 15th IEEE International Conference on Communication Technology*, pp. 26–31. Nov 2013.

[90] A. J. Duncan, S. Creese, and M. Goldsmith. "Insider Attacks in Cloud Computing." In *2012 IEEE 11th International Conference on Trust, Security and Privacy in Computing and Communications*, pp. 857–862. June 2012.

[91] M. Bharati and S. Tamane. "Intrusion detection systems (IDS) future challenges in cloud based environment." In *2017 1st International Conference on Intelligent Systems and Information Management (ICISIM)*, pp. 240–250. Oct 2017.

[92] C. DeCusatis, P. Liengtiraphan, A. Sager, and M. Pinelli. "Implementing Zero Trust Cloud Networks with Transport Access Control and First Packet Authentication." In *2016 IEEE International Conference on Smart Cloud (SmartCloud)*, pp. 5–10. Nov 2016.

[93] V. Mahajan and S. K. Peddoju. "Deployment of Intrusion Detection System in Cloud: A Performance-Based Study." In *2017 IEEE Trustcom/BigDataSE/ICESS*, pp. 1103–1108. Aug 2017.

[94] C. P. Garrido. "Lightweight Container-Based OpenEPC Deployment and its Evaluation.", 2016. URL `https://pdfs.semanticscholar.org/presentation/b71d/93d0c691b3ccb3b77cf1ad4b79be2724e98f.pdf`.

[95] Y. Yiakoumis and M. Kobayashi. "Innovating in Your Network with OpenFlow: A Hands-on Tutorial." In *2010 18th IEEE Symposium on High Performance Interconnects*, pp. 121–122. Aug 2010.

[96] A. Sheoran, X. Bu, L. Cao, P. Sharma, and S. Fahmy. "An empirical case for container-driven fine-grained VNF resource flexing." In *2016 IEEE Conference on Network Function Virtualization and Software Defined Networks (NFV-SDN)*, pp. 121–127. Nov 2016.

[97] R. Izard. "How to Work with Fast-Failover OpenFlow Groups.", 2016. URL https://floodlight.atlassian.net/wiki/display/floodlightcontroller/How+to+Work+with+Fast-Failover+OpenFlow+Groups.

[98] J. Sun, K. Sun, and Q. Li. "CyberMoat: Camouflaging critical server infrastructures with large scale decoy farms." In *2017 IEEE Conference on Communications and Network Security (CNS)*, pp. 1–9. Oct 2017.

[99] Y. Grunenberger. "docker-openairinterface-epc.", 2018. URL https://github.com/ravens/docker-openairinterface-epc.

[100] Y. Grunenberger. "docker-openairinterface-enb.", 2018. URL https://github.com/ravens/docker-openairinterface-enb.

[101] M. Peuster. "Containernet: Mininet fork that allows to use Docker containers as hosts in emulated networks.", 2018. URL https://github.com/containernet/containernet.

[102] N. Gude, T. Koponen, J. Pettit, B. Pfaff, M. Casado, N. McKeown, and S. Shenker. "NOX: Towards an Operating System for Networks." *SIGCOMM Comput. Commun. Rev.*, vol. 38, no. 3, pp. 105–110, Jul. 2008. URL http://doi.acm.org/10.1145/1384609.1384625.

[103] O. Salman, I. H. Elhajj, A. Kayssi, and A. Chehab. "SDN controllers: A comparative study." In *2016 18th Mediterranean Electrotechnical Conference (MELECON)*, pp. 1–6. April 2016.

[104] S. Shirali-Shahreza and Y. Ganjali. "Efficient Implementation of Security Applications in OpenFlow Controller with FleXam." In *2013 IEEE 21st Annual Symposium on High-Performance Interconnects*, pp. 49–54. Aug 2013.

# Appendix A

# SDN architectural breakdown

Figure A.1 shows the three main layers of the SDN architecture as well as the interfaces between each layer. The following appendix describes each element from a top down perspective.

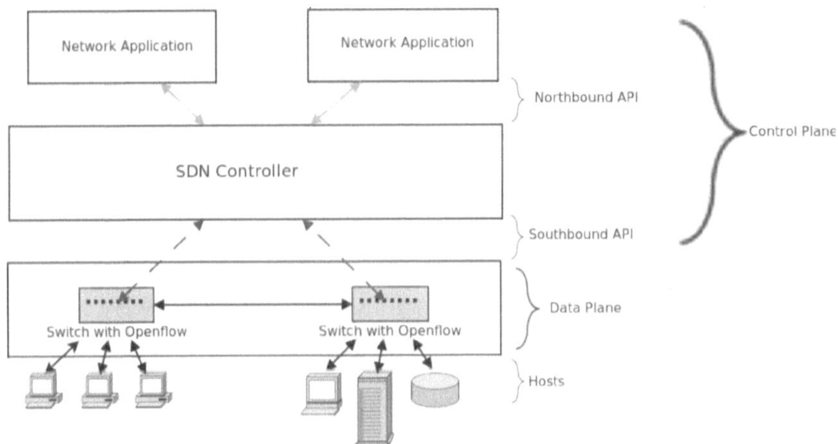


Figure A.1: SDN architecture

## A.1 Network Applications

The network applications contain the overarching business goals and policies that are required of the network, and determine the forwarding state that should be applied to the forwarding elements of the network. Common goals of the network applications are isolation, routing, security, load balancing and traffic engineering [79]. Many NOS distributions contain built in applications that deal with common network functionalities. Applications are preferably built in a micro-service fashion where each application has one specific function, this modularity allows for the applications to be reused in different combinations[103].

Most popular NOSes are open source, therefore allowing users to make alterations to the internal functionalities of the controller to fit specific needs. This allows for applications to be developed at a faster rate by the users of the systems when compared to having specific vendors acting as a bottle neck in terms of innovation.

## A.2 Northbound API

The northbound API is the interface between NOS and the network applications. Through the northbound API the network applications are able to install the flow rules they deem necessary via the abstraction and functionalities provided by the NOS. The northbound API is also necessary to get notifications to the applications when the state of the network has been updated.

Current controllers have at least two different types of northbound APIs. The first is an internal programmatic interface which is controller specific. Applications making use of this interface need to be written in the same language as the controller and essentially act as add on modules to the NOS. This interface allows for the applications to read network state and be updated with topology changes to the network as soon as the controller makes the changes. This approach is useful as the applications can then interact with the controller with all the methods built into the programming language as well as allowing for applications to have real-time updates of new information available to the controller.

The second type of Northbound API interface that controllers provide is a REpresentational State Transfer (REST) API. REST is a common web development architectural style that makes use of the HyperText Transfer Protocol (HTTP) in order for client and server to communicate. Current controllers have similar REST interfaces therefore applications can be created to run across a vast array of controllers without needing to be ported to individual controllers. The downside of the REST API is the fact that the applications would constantly need to be polling the NOS for updates to the network state as the NOS does not allow for REST applications to subscribe to updates on network state changes. This can lead to a significant delay before the application can act on updates as well as wastefully utilising processing overhead while the applications constantly poll for updates.

## A.3   SDN controller

The NOS or network controller abstracts the complexities of the network management away from applications in a similar way to how a computer operating system abstracts the hardware interface complexities from computer applications [102]. The primary purpose of the NOS is to abstract away the specifics of controlling individual network devices as well as providing essential services and functionalities to the network. Examples of these services and functionalities include installing forwarding rules on the data forwarding elements, network state and topology monitoring, distributing configuration adjustments to the network and device discovery.

The NOS is critical to the SDN architecture and the NOS selected for the network must accommodate all the requirements of the network. As there are different types of networks that may require a NOS, there have been many different types of NOSes developed with a wide range of performance characteristics, architectures and built in services and functionalities. When selecting which NOS to use for a network the following need to be taken into consideration:

- Supported Northbound API

- Supported Southbound API (OpenFlow version)

- Architecture

- Modularity

- Industry partners

- Existing Network Applications

- Built in feature set

- Documentation

- Intended Application Domain

- Centralised or Distributed

Table A.1: Feature comparison of three popular Network Operating Systems

| | Northbound APIs | Southbound APIs | Base architecture | Modularity | Intended Application | Centralised or Distributed |
|---|---|---|---|---|---|---|
| ODL | REST API | OF 1.0, 1.3 and 1.4 SNMP, BGP/LS, PCEP, LISP, NETCONF/YANG | Java | High | Data Centre | Distributed |
| ONOS | REST API | OF 1.0 and 1.3, NETCONF | Java | High | WAN and Carrier networks | Distributed |
| RYU | REST API | OF 1.0, 1.2, 1.3, 1.4, NETCONF, OFCONFIG | Python | Moderate | Research and Campus networks | Centralised |

There are three notable NOSes to mention, first is Opendaylight (ODL) which is designed for the data-centre. Next is ONOS which was originally designed for use in carrier networks. RYU is the third NOS and is highly relevant to this work as it is primarily used in research and development purposes [103]. The targeted networks for each of the NOSes highly affects the architecture of the controller as well as the available network applications.

## A.4  Southbound API

The Southbound interface connects the NOS and data forwarding elements (switches). Through the southbound API, the NOS is able to gather a global network view from the switches, collect statistics on traffic and install forwarding rules onto the switches. OpenFlow, ForCES and NetConf are all different southbound APIs that can be supported by NOSes. OpenFlow is the most commonly used southbound API although most controllers can support more than one southbound API.

OpenFlow is a protocol that provides abstraction for a forwarding pipeline by providing a standard and open interface for the communication between NOS and data forwarding elements. OpenFlow is an open source protocol so it is highly modular and configurable to cater for specific requirements. This design is a deviation from the previously vendor specific network languages that switches communicated with, therefore ushering in the ability for active open-source development within the field.

The standardisation and open source nature of the OpenFlow protocol is particularly useful to network operators as vendor lock in is a non factor. If the switch is able to communicate using OpenFlow then it can be substituted by another switch that has the OpenFlow protocol included in its design, no matter which vendor or open source project developed it [79].

## A.5  Data Forwarding Elements

The lowest level of the SDN architecture are the data forwarding elements, or switches. These elements are responsible for forwarding traffic through the network based on their forwarding tables installed by the NOS. The switches also collect statistics from the network and relay these back to the controller. The switches are able to communicate via protocols such as OpenFlow discussed above. OpenFlow 1.3 is most implemented version of the protocol [97] and even though later versions have been released, 1.3 is still has the highest support amongst vendors [103].

OpenFlow 1.3 switches contain one or more flow tables [79], when a packet is received by the switch the packet gets processed by a data processing pipeline against the entries in the flow tables. The flow tables contain multiple flow entries, each flow entry consists of traffic statistics, packet matching rules and actions to apply to the matching packets. Actions that can be specified to be applied to packets include forwarding, dropping or modifying. Packets can be forwarded to a flow table, a port or to the controller in the case the the flow is not found in the flow table. The ability to modify flows as well as sending the packets onto the controller are of particular interest to this research as malicious flows would be unknown in the typical use case of the network. Once the controller and applications have decided on an action to take the flow would could be modified to a different node as opposed to the initial target of the malicious flow.

# Appendix B

# NFV Breakdown

NFV introduces the ability to automatically deploy network functions [37]. With NFV, all EPC components are able to be virtualised as specific Virtual Network Functions (VNFs). This has come from the need to scale networks without relying on proprietary hardware which is a cumbersome and expensive exercise. Some of the main benefits of the NFV architecture are as follows:

- Ease of management of network functions during their full life cycle

- Ability to deploy functions automatically and scale existing functions up. Both horizontal and vertical scaling.

- Reducing energy consumption

- Lowering the Capital expenditure (CAPEX) by moving functionality from dedicated hardware boxes into virtual resources (ie containers or virtual machines)

- Lowering Operating Expenditures by not needing specialist staff or relying on the vendor of the middle-box for maintenance or configuration changes on network functions.

- Cost efficient and quick deployment of network functions.

# Appendix C

# VMs vs Containers

Linux based containers have been around for more than 20 years, but it has only been since the introduction of Docker in 2013 that container based virtualisation has taken off in the world of computer sciences. VMs allow for the creation of fully virtualised environments including separate kernels per instance. Whereas containers are seen as more lightweight, with each instance utilising the host machine's kernel and libraries [96]. The container approach is shown to utilise resources more efficiently due to the lower overhead costs per instance deployment [74, 75]. These differences are detailed in Figure C.1 below specifically for the Docker containerisation platform.

Table C.1 details the quantitative differences between container and VM based implementations of the OpenEPC [94]. The averages were calculated on the four specific logical nodes of the OpenEPC that are required for basic functionality to be achieved i.e., HSS, MME, SGW and PGW. The average deploy times were measured when deploying individual instances on the test bed.

Table C.1: Comparison of Container vs VM implementations of the OpenEPC

| VNF deployment method | Average Image Size (MB) | Average Memory Usage (MB) | Average Time to Deploy (seconds) |
| --- | --- | --- | --- |
| Virtual Machine | 1352 | 3.68 | 16 |
| Container (Docker) | 368 | 0.975 | 3 |

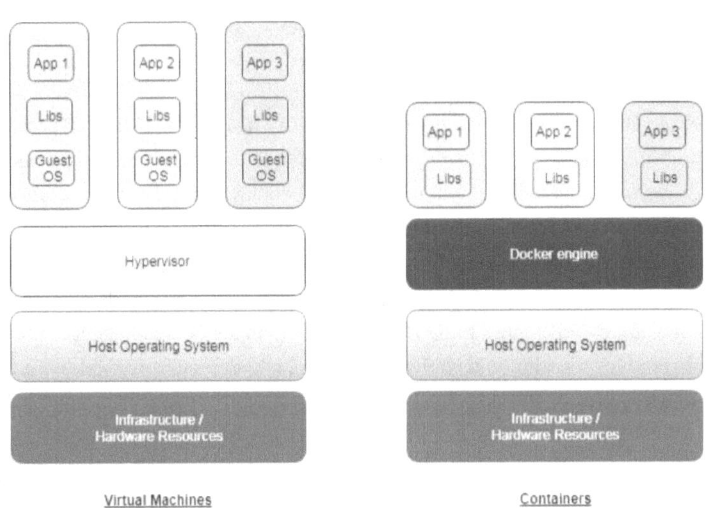


Figure C.1: VM vs Docker container architecture

# Appendix D

# Containernet Breakdown

Containernet is an open source extension of the popular Mininet project. The Mininet base provides a system that is able to emulate a network using lightweight process-based virtualisation to deploy virtual switches, virtual Ethernet links and virtual hosts within a single Linux VM [95]. Containernet extends this functionality with the ability to deploy containers as the hosts within the emulated network, while still being backwards compatible with Mininet and maintaining the same design goals of achieving a platform that is able to scalably, flexibly and realistically deploy a network on a developers laptop.

Figure D.1 shows the architecture of Containernet. The sequence of steps followed to get a network up inside the emulator as well as being able to interact with all parts of the network are as follows. First the developer defines the network topology, for this a python script was written that calls the Containernet python API (1). As part of this network definition script, the virtual switches can be configured to communicate with a remote controller that is running as process separate from Containernet (2). VNFs and virtual switches are then deployed in the Mininet-based emulation environment including virtual Ethernet links to connect the network nodes together to one another (3). Once the VNFs, vSwitches and virtual links are deployed, developers can then interact with all parts of the network via Containernet's

interactive CLI, this can allow developers to carry out any process on any of
the hosts, whether they are Docker containers or virtual hosts (4).

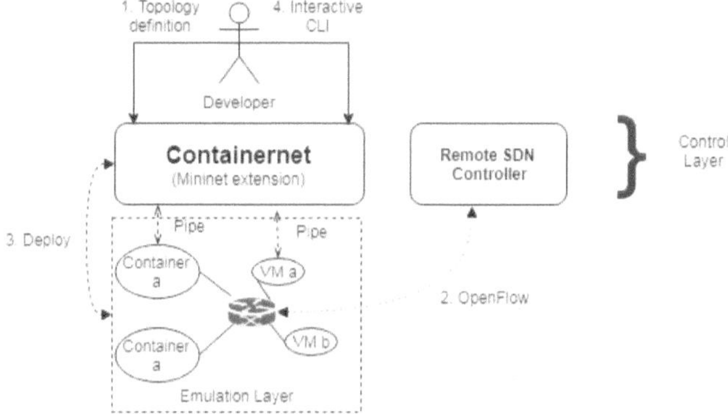


Figure D.1: Containernet architecture with remote SDN controller

# Appendix E

# Technical Description of NIPS Setup and Evaluation

In order to get to the state where the NIPS application can be evaluated, the following technical steps needed to be followed to get the network environment setup correctly. All the following steps were run in individual bash terminals on the base Ubuntu 18.04 OS.

The first step was to run the NIPS application as a extra module to the RYU controller. This was done by using the Python package installer (pip) to install the RYU controller and run the NIPS application module using the newly installed 'ryu-manager' to run the python script that contains the NIPS application. This running NIPS application extension of the RYU controller can be seen in Figure E.1. When the application is being run, the RYU controller is listening on port 6633 for OpenFlow communications.

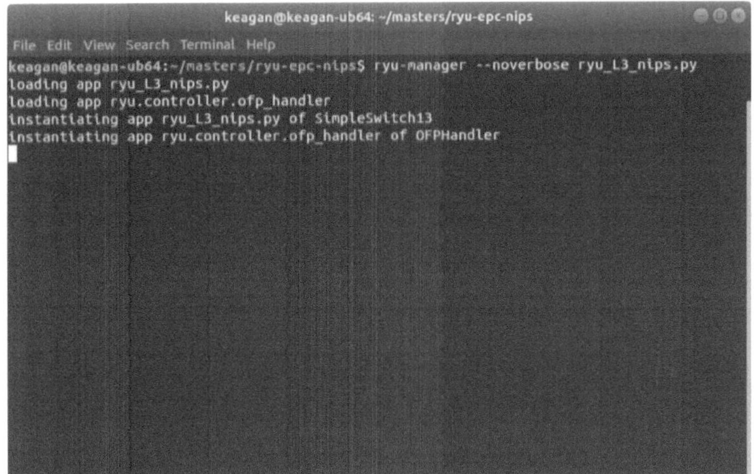

Figure E.1: RYU manager running the NIPS application as a module extension for the RYU controller

Next step was to get the Containernet emulation environment up with the correct topology. Containernet was installed using the instructions on the Github page found in [101]. That installation ensures that all the correct Python libraries are included for Containernet to run correctly. A script can now be run that details the topology of the network using the Python process as can be seen in Figure E.2. The script being run creates a topology as seen in Figure 4.4 with the OVS instance connecting to the RYU controller deployed in the first step above. This script also performs all the path checks along the critical paths needed for the EPC to be functioning correctly.

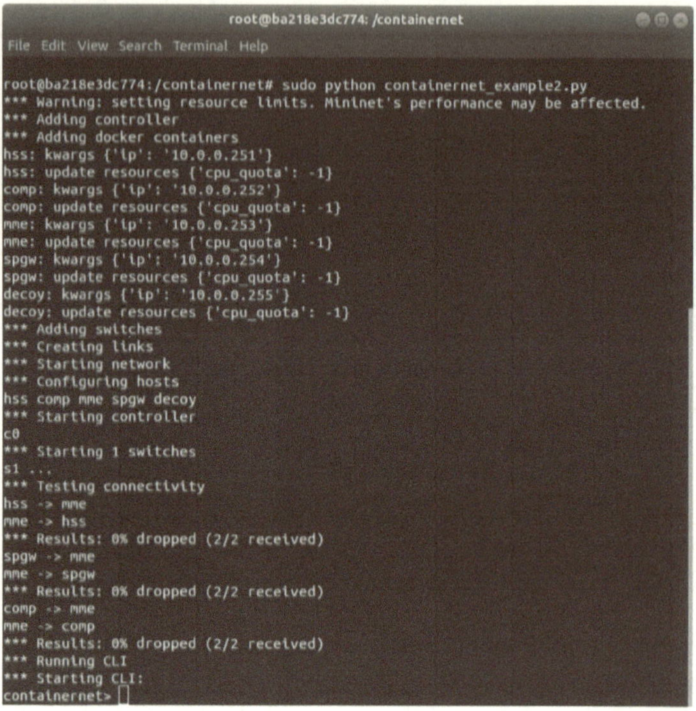

Figure E.2: Containernet setting up the network topology used for evaluation

The containerised OpenEPC needed to be run in the Containernet environment. In order to get all the Docker images setup correctly to deploy all the container VNFs, the Github page found in [99] details how to obtain all the OpenEPC container VNFs. The enodeB emulator was found on a separate repository by the same author [100]. Once all these images were loaded, they were deployed in Containernet as can be seen in the lines following "***  Adding docker containers" in Figure E.2.

The Containernet CLI was used from this point onwards to validate the NIPS application. This interaction with the hosts/containers in the Contain-